# The WITCH I Am
### Volume One

From Darkness to Understanding - A Journey of Mediumship

MARIA DORGAN WRITING AS

# MARIE F CROW

# Copyright

THE WITCH I AM
Copyright © 2023 by Marie F Crow

All rights reserved.

Formatting & Cover Design by KP Designs
- www.kpdesignshop.com
Published by Kingston Publishing Company
- www.kingstonpublishing.com

No portion of this book may be reproduced in any form without written permission from the publisher or author, except as permitted by U.S. copyright law. The uploading, scanning, and distribution of this book in any form or by any means — including but not limited to electronic, mechanical, photocopying, recording, or otherwise — without the permission of the copyright holder is illegal and punishable by law. Please purchase only authorized editions of this work, and do not participate in or encourage electronic piracy of copyrighted materials. Your support of the author's rights is appreciated.

## Table of Contents

Copyright ........................................................................................... 3
Table of Contents ............................................................................. 5
Section One – The Discovery ........................................................ 9
Section Two – The Survival .......................................................... 27
Section Three – The Late Bloomers ............................................ 45
Section Four – Your Spiritual Team ............................................ 53
Section Five – Leaning into Your New Life ............................... 99
Section Six – Now What? ............................................................ 108
Section Seven – The Road is Now Open .................................. 115
Appendix ........................................................................................ 119
About the Author ......................................................................... 132
Also by the Author ....................................................................... 133
Podcast ........................................................................................... 135
Where to find the Author? .......................................................... 136
About the Publisher ..................................................................... 137

A wise friend once told me the hardest journey one could ever take is the journey of self-discovery because it is the one journey which will shred you to the bone, put those bones on display and then scatter them to the winds of change. It's the one journey one can never turn back on once it begins.

Are you ready to go on that journey? This book has been written, not for me, but for you, so that you may find the courage to take the first steps upon that hard journey we all must go through in life, or else be doomed to live forever in the shadows of our own failed potential.

# Section One – The Discovery

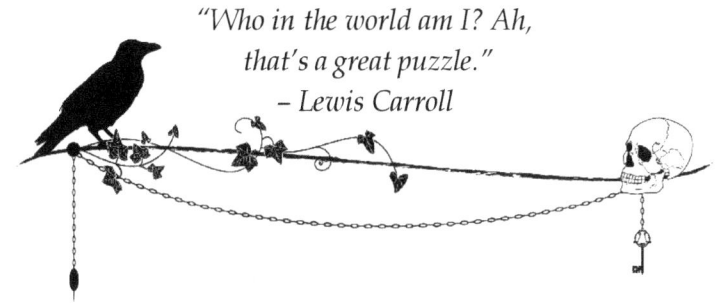

*"Who in the world am I? Ah, that's a great puzzle."*
– Lewis Carroll

One of the questions I get asked the most is – when did you know you could do all this? It's a question which always comes with a pause and lump in my throat. It's not a simple answer.

Growing up, I have always had 'imaginary friends'. I could see them just as whole, and real, as I would see you if you were sitting near me right now. Each had their own personalities, needs and time spent together because none of them ever stayed for long. My 'friends' would appear one day and then be gone the next. It was exceedingly rare if any of them were to last for more than a few days. I think the longest was Kent.

Kent was an elderly gentleman. I can still see his mahogany pipe and smell its sweet tobacco. I remember his red flannel shirt with its uneven black blocks. His jeans were always stained around the knees and the hem touching his well-worn black work boots. He let me know from the very first conversation he was there to watch over me. To him, this was a job he failed at when he was living. Watching over me as a child brought him to the light, the peace most souls are looking for to be able to finally, fully, cross over. He stayed by my bed on nights when I cried myself to sleep. He was there to warn me about school bullies. He held my hand when I desperately needed it.

In time, he moved on, but to this day, there is nothing as comforting as red flannel and I have often reached for mine on days when I just need that little extra something to get through the day.

My parents never really understood what I meant when I would try to tell them about those who would visit me. To them, it was something I was going to outgrow. In time, they would become highly creative about how to force me to do just that. Before that though, it was a game. They would often ask me to guess items in boxes or tell them something about an event, or a person. What was amusing, quickly became alarming to them. When the names of my 'friends' started striking a little too close to the heart, long talks would take place about how cruel it was to make fun of situations in such a way. Being a child eager to please those around me, this was very confusing.

I would often be told I was making up things, or lying to hurt people. It wasn't possible for me to know things about deceased family members, but I did. My 'friends' would eagerly aid me in collecting any answers put before me. They provided most of my answers at that age as I still was not aware of what I was doing, much less to reach beyond the souls in front of me and to a higher source for my information. Being a child, a source of pure love and light, as most children are, the souls who gathered around me at that time were also of love and light. I didn't have any reason to doubt their answers or their genuine interest in helping me. Now, trained and certified in many different forms of mediumship, I know how lucky I was as a child to have only those souls gathered around me. It could have been much different. Unfortunately, it didn't remain this way for long.

As the abuse began to intensify, so did my mediumship. Simply holding my hand was no longer enough to help my light survive what I was enduring at that time. When one encounters nothing but darkness, their light will also fade. Mine had started too rapidly dim.

I will not go into depth about the abuse. The acts of those who abused me do not define me today any more than the abuse itself does as to who I am. It is only part of the explanation. The acts the adults did supplied a lesson for me, a trial by fire, if you will. The only importance of the abuse inflicted is that it allowed me to explore my natural gifts in ways few will experience, putting me on the path of teacher and healer. None the less, as my home life became increasingly unstable, my abilities grew.

Statistically, I should not be alive today. Most who endured what I did have fallen to the wayside, lost to those who loved them forever through the many forms of addiction and suicide. I came close to joining those numbers. I believe my mediumship saved me.

During the worst of the abuse, I stumbled upon, quite literally, trance mediumship. I didn't understand what it was at that time. The souls who kept me company knew I would not mentally, or spiritually, survive for much longer. The first night I slipped away from the confinement of my body, it was terrifying. I had no professional training or understanding of what I was doing then. My abilities already held the understanding of it, and without knowing it, the need to escape from what was happening triggered the ability.

I remember floating above my body, watching what was being done. Just like the protective souls they were, a woman came rushing towards me, placing her hands over my eyes, before pulling me from the room. I can still hear her voice to this day sometimes when I go under, telling me to give trust to the process. At the time, the only thing I gave trust to was her, not the floating sensation or the separation from my body. That was pure terror.

The souls would take turns slipping in and out of my body, allowing the adult to believe I was still there. For as long as the abuse lasted there were willing souls to intervene, stealing me away from the experience. While they held the empty shell of my body, I was far away, walking in meadows and forests with who I now know as one of my oldest Guides. She kept my soul safe as it traveled away but she was never far behind me. We had grand tea parties filled with more cakes than sandwiches. We swam in lakes of vibrant colors. Sometimes we would simply sit in the dark as she coached me through life and the lessons I was being taught about adults. She was doing her best to keep the light inside me more than just a flickering ember, but unfortunately, Guides can only direct us, they can't do it for us. Her direction I was starting to doubt, falling prey to the darker side of mediumship.

Though my 'friends' did their best to protect me, the dead have their limits and they had found theirs. I might not have memory of the whole event, but my body held the aftermath. There was nothing anyone could do about that. Nor could they protect me from harsh words of those who were supposed to protect me. The constant chipping away at my body and mind took its toll. It wasn't hard for darker energies to find their way into my presence. Up until then, I was only surrounded by those souls who wished to help in exchange for a message delivered or just acknowledgement to their presence. In my naivety, I began to listen to the voices of spirits who only wanted to harm me. It was these spirits who coached me how to release the pain I was feeling by carving into my own flesh their names, as acknowledgement, since I was at this point not allowed to talk about my 'friends' anymore. It was also under the instructions of these spirits my first suicide attempt was made. They had removed the good souls from me and had even began taking their place when I slipped away. I was becoming everything mediums are taught from which to protect themselves, but since I had no guidance, only darkness, the darkness was winning.

It was at this point in my life where the diagnosis of schizophrenia and multiple personality disorder was placed upon me – a label which would define how I was treated for a long time. The abuse was never correlated to my behavior. The abuser knew well how to manage any questions put before him. It was easier to blame the victim than to admit to what was happening in my home, and thanks to a very misguided family therapist, my family now had that possibility.

I was the problem. My 'friends' were the problem. My lies and manipulation of emotions was the problem. Thus, in my mind, as was the desired goal, my mediumship was the problem. The very tool which I had used to survive was wrong, sinful, and disgusting. It must be stopped. *I* must be stopped.

At this point, my parents were happy to commit me to one mental hospital or another. Sometimes, after a round of trance mediumship, I would awaken to a bed in the E.R. as I waited for transport due to psychotic behavior. We never talked about the reason for the behavior. Afterall, the problem was me.

I would go through in-depth therapy session to retrain how I dealt with my life – since bringing up the abuse was forbidden, and an excuse. I was the problem. When souls would arrive, and there were plenty in the facilities to find me, I was instructed to harm myself to associate this behavior with negative consequences. From pinching myself, to rubber band snaps, even pills whose whole purpose was to sour anything I would eat for hours, was given upon their arrival. My young mind twisted this amazing ability into something to fear and hate about myself. This resulted in a deeper depression as I cut off the source of healing in my life. I literally cut away a piece of me, shutting the doors I didn't know had been opened for me.

I would become a very awkward child, having very few friends because I was afraid to reveal too much. Even though the door was shut, souls would still find me. I might not see them, but I could feel their presence sending me into the perverted training which has been allowed to be administered. I would embrace the darkness because I could not escape the shame instilled in me. Cutting became my main outlet and the suicide attempts would continue.

So why do you need to know all this? What does this have to do with *your* journey? What can the trauma of a little girl long into her teens help you understand about *your own* journey?

Most people discover their abilities by accident. The doors are often swung wide open after surviving something awful, leaving the person even more confused than they already are by life and her lessons. Without any understanding of what is happening, we start to question our sanity. *"Am I going crazy?"* we often ask during these moments, allowing doubt and negative talk to override the process. How many of you, yourself, have asked that question when suddenly feeling like a loved one is near or knowing the answer to something you have no knowledge about? See how slippery that slope can be? We'll cover more on this later.

For those who are, as Lady GaGa would sing, *BornTthis Way*, you have to understand just because those around you at the time didn't understand what was happening doesn't mean it wasn't real. We have to give grace and space to those who harmed us if that harm was done without knowledge. Now, I hope your treatment wasn't as harsh as mine as a child, but if it was, forgive yourself for hating who you are and then give those who harmed you space to heal themselves. You don't have to forgive those who harmed you. That's a personal choice. You do though have to give those people the space so they can work through their own healing. Perhaps, in time, you will reconcile when both parties are in a healthy spot. This is also a great moment for parents with children who are showing signs of awareness. You don't have to understand what your child is going through. You just have to have compassion and understanding. There are plenty of spiritual coaches out there who can step in to guide your child to healthy boundaries with Spirit and their abilities. Just listening to your child, believing in what they are telling you, is an amazing lesson in life you can provide. It will help them understand as they grow that people are different and that doesn't mean they are any less than another person because of that fact.

Not all parents are excited when their children start to express their experiences. Nor are all children happy to be experiencing them. The first step is for both the parent and the child to sit down, talk honestly about what is going on, and together decide how everyone wants to handle the experiences. This is not something one can just turn off like a bad habit. Much like the color of their hair or eyes, or the little quirk the child does that you have come to love, this is a part of the child. It may fade or intensify, but it will never truly go away.

Instill in your child you are there for them. They can come to you. You are eager and ready to listen to them. Even if the idea of your child being a medium doesn't thrill you, you must put aside your own opinions. Children can pick up on our slightest mood change. If they sense you becoming upset with them when they come to you, they will stop talking and that could lead to more trouble as they figure out how to navigate this on their own.

You wouldn't leave your child to fail math because they don't understand the concepts. You would hire a tutor. Why would you leave them to figure something like this out on their own?

Luckily, with the rise of Spiritualism there are more resources available now for parents then there were for mine. Leaving people lost for resources as we once were, this is no longer such a taboo topic. There are many different avenues now for classification and education upon the subject. Even religious leaders now offer classes to understand mediumship. Leave the choice of guidance to your child. Afterall, it's them who will be undergoing the process. Your job is to be the best back up dancer you can be for your child. So, get those dancing shoes out!

If you think your child is showing signs of mediumship, or just being open to the spiritual plane, I have supplied some exercises on the following pages. Remember, open dialog, an open heart and an open mind are the best tools to have moving forward for you and your child.

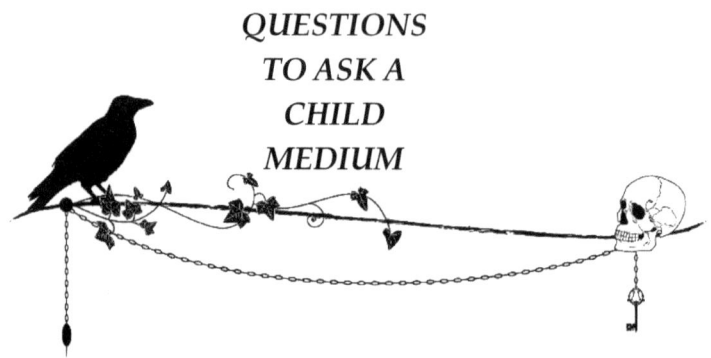

## QUESTIONS TO ASK A CHILD MEDIUM

1. Can you tell me what the person you're seeing looks like?

*Write this information down. Compare the information to any passed relative who may be visiting from the other side. Often times, our departed will visit our children because they are more open to their arrival than we are as adults. This is normal! We also want to take note if the person is changing in appearances or if it is different people all the time.*

2. How do you feel when this person is near you?

*Your child will know instinctively if this person is good or bad. Let them be honest about how they feel. Don't judge them for thinking harshly. This is how their little minds rationalize their emotions. Now is not the time to explain because someone looks scary doesn't mean they are. Since at this time we don't know the true intent behind this spirit, it is best to not over evaluate it.*

3. Do you like it when this person is around?

*This is where your guidance will shine. Once again, manners are not the teaching tool at this juncture. If the answer is a 'no', let the answer be no. We as mediums should never feel forced to interact with a spirit which we do not want around. The child needs to understand this as soon as possible. Let the child know it is perfectly okay to tell the spirit no, to go away and it's fine to refuse to interact with the spirit. Teaching your child right away that their space is sacred, and spirits must have permission to enter it, will be setting them on an unbreakable foundation for their future as a medium. If the child is uncomfortable in standing up for themselves, a great friend of mine once told me 'no' is a complete sentence. Let them know the word 'no' is enough.*

4.  Is there anything this person asks you to do or talks about?

*If your child told you they were suddenly talking to any adult, you would ask this. It's the same concept with spirits. As a parent, you need to know any adult who your child is interacting with, what their conversations are about, what they want from your child. Are they trying to convince your child to do something harmful? Are they empowering your child? Even if you do not understand exactly what the child is going through, you, as the adult, must still be guarding the child from danger. Listen without reaction to what your child tells you. Help them work through if this spirit is best for them to be interacting with at this time. Then come up with a game plan you can do together to handle the situation.*

5. Is there anything I can do for you?

*The answer, most likely, will be no. That's not the point of the question. The question is there to let the child know you are there for them. Which are often times the most transformational question you could ask.*

## *TEACHING YOUR CHILD HOW TO REMOVE SPIRIT*

There will be times when a spirit will come through whom your child does not want to interact with at this time. There are simple ways to help your child to do this. I will guide you through it below.

To fully interact with spirit, one must reach an alpha state of mind, or meditative state. This is where your mind slows down, rests, and allows the spiritual realm to reach through in vivid clarity. To help your child reach this state of mind, teach them how to slow their breathing, how to reach a calm meditative state. Do not over complicate this. It will only add to their anxiety, making it harder to reach the state of mind.

When they have relaxed, ask them to invite the spirit forward to talk with you.

Ask your child to let you know when the spirit has arrived, letting your child know you are right there with them through this entire process. You won't leave them. You're doing this together.

When you are notified the spirit has arrived encourage your child to be firm and tell the spirit they no longer wish for this spirit to be in their space. In fact, use the words 'not allowed'. Encourage them to be firm. Shout it if they feel the need to for the message to be fully heard. Allow your child to take charge of this moment, expressing what is allowed and what won't be tolerated any longer. Your child is the boss at this moment, and you are there to enforce and encourage.

After the exchange, help your child return to the alpha state once again.

Now ask your child to invite a spirit they trust to step closer. This may be a departed loved one or even their Guardian Angels. Call them by name so they know to come.

When your child notifies you this person has arrived, have them ask this person to help with the removal of the spirit your child no longer wants around them. Ask for their protection and blessings in this endeavor. Our loved ones on the other side are an amazing source of help and guidance for our lives. Let them be this now, offering your child the warmth and protection family can provide.

Thank them for their assistance and have your child return to a conscious state, trusting the spirit will be handled by those who are there to protect them.

This process might have to be repeated a few times until you can find a Spiritual Coach to help customize the approach. Assure your child each time the process is completed, the stronger your child will become in their abilities and their boundaries. Spirits, like humans, sometimes need to be told a few times what the rules are before they learn them. We all know a person like this in our lives!

## ITEMS TO HELP PROTECT YOUR CHILD

There are many different items you can add around your house to help protect your child while their abilities are being understood. Remember, this is your child's experience. They should always be involved in choosing any items which are selected to help them. They will 'know' what items will help them the most.

****

### Grounding Crystals

Hematite, Obsidian, Onyx, Smokey Quartz, Black Tourmaline, and my favorite, Shungite. They may be worn or placed around the home or even both. They will work the same.

****

### Easy Protection Barriers

Smoke cleansing: visit your nearest metaphysical store to be sure you are buying high quality items. They can recommend the best options for your needs from what they have in stock. This technique will purify your home, chasing away anything negative which is trying to invade your space. Allow this to be another way for you and your child to bond over what they are experiencing, showing them that you are just as invested in figuring this out and are there to protect them. In essence, you are putting the foundation of belief in your child.

\*\*\*\*
## *Bells*

Hang chimes near doors and windows to clear away residual negative energy. Place small bells beside beds to be rung after bad dreams or when feeling a negative presence. This will also serve to alert you when your child needs your protection.

\*\*\*\*
## *Favorite Huggable Toy*

Stuffed toys have been used for many varied reasons surrounding anxiety, and honestly, that's the best way to think of this situation. Introducing this item will help your small child to deal with their guests when you are not able to be around your child. This will allow them to have a sense of protection and also a way to handle any souls who may find them when they are about their day. I often teach two different approaches to doing this. One, the child who is secure in the experiences can tell the souls to speak with the toy, and not them, when they are doing their normal day. Of course, the spirits won't actually talk to the toy. They will get the hint though their presence is not wanted at this time. Two, they can hug the toy tightly until the soul goes away. Unfortunately, this doesn't work for school age children as often they are not allowed to have toys at their desks, but option one does still allow them to practice the techniques of setting ground rules with those who visit them.

\*\*\*\*

There are many ways to set your child on a solid path as a medium. There are just as many different ideas and perspectives on the topic, too. Holding over thirty different forms of certification, I can only speak about what I have been offered allowing me to form my honest thoughts on the subject. These thoughts come from not only the many classes and lectures I have attended, but also from being a child trying to understand it all. I have met many mediums in my travels who have had solid structure and understanding from their parents when their abilities were discovered. These mediums are confident in ways I am almost always jealous over. They have their inner light secure inside themselves, unwavering and unbreakable. Their boundaries are protected, saving them from risks being a medium can sometimes bring to our lives. All of this is due to having a family support system willing and able to nurture and have faith in them.

    I encourage you to be this support, building an amazing life for your child of love and light, and most importantly, security. After all, isn't that all we want for our children? Jobs, spouses, heartache, and victory will eventually find them, but if they have stable ground to travel upon, the ground you created for them, there is nothing which will break them.

## INVOKING PROTECTION

Come up with a special chant, or prayer, for your child to repeat when needing protection. This is their special request for help from deceased loved ones and their Guides and Guardians. Have them always repeat this three times to help settle their protection around them. This can be a simple sentence or as in depth as you both feel is necessary. Do not over complicate it for the child will need to have this in hand or memorized to be used easily and often. You can also have the child imagine a bubble of white light encasing them. Envision this light fully surrounding them, pushing away all spiritual threats. Expand the light further and further until the child feels fully protected. This bubble may stay as long as the child needs it to, keeping them safe.

# Section Two – The Survival

*"But what he'd shown me about myself wasn't glamorous. It was worrying. It was something I had to change. And luckily, he'd show me the way."*
*– Danny Wallace*

The opening of gifts, or discovery of them for those who are not born with them, often happens in times of turmoil, stress, tension, and intense change, as mentioned in the last section. Nothing throws all of those things together in such a made for television style like the tween and teen years provide for us. There's a reason most young adult themed shows, movies and books are situated around someone finally discovering who they are in the paranormal world. This is the age when we are struggling to separate ourselves from our parents' ideas to find our own identity. And, do I dare say, magically this is when closed doors are flung open.

Now, before we all exhale and think to ourselves that if it hasn't happened by my twenties, it won't happen. That's not true. At all. Life doesn't keep her trauma to just when we are young. She spreads that out evenly throughout our lives. Maybe she just hasn't found you yet, or she has, and we just haven't made it to your section, yet. Either way, the doors are always there. Timing and acceptance are all that is waiting for you.

Back to the tween and teen years. This is the time in our lives when we start to really figure out where we want our lives to head. In some ways, we are starting on a plan, or path. One we may change several times, but it's a start.

We are searching for what we believe as normal, even if it is not someone else's idea of normal. The word normal though isn't about just blending in. It's about feeling safe, seen and appreciated by those who are also looking for the same normal. Amid peers who are also starting to divide and clique up, it's terrifying for most to feel as if they don't have that normal. Those of us with gifts, it can be worse. It isn't always understood how we know Jeremy is cheating on Jenny with Jessica. We just do. Try explaining that one and still keeping your friends. The natural thing to do is to not talk, not tell, not admit when the voices, or the sensations, are around. But then, is it your normal?

Kids with gifts often will start to isolate themselves. So afraid they may anger their peers or be ridiculed they will seclude themselves from their families, friends, life in general, just to avoid the consequences of being who they truly are. Which is tragic because while an artist may be raved about for their gifts, these children are shunned and mocked for theirs. Sometimes, the biggest culprits of this are not their peers. It's their families.

As glossed over before, my family was not aware of how to handle my abilities or, much less, the darker aspects of spiritual interaction. Not only was I unable to find my normal due to the abuse, but being able to hear secrets, see energy shifts when someone was lying and seeing spirits all around me made it even more difficult to find my group of peers and friends. I was groomed by my abuser to smile and always act that everything is okay. Meanwhile, I am living in a ring of purgatory with no one to confide in. This is when, and I fully believe to this day, the demonic entities found me.

Those of us who can sense spirit have little 'hello's when spirit is around. It might be a feeling, a sound, sometimes even a smell to let us know who and when someone has decided to step forward. We use these little signals to be able to identify familiar spirits from new spirits making their presence known. During this time in my life, and sometimes still if I allow myself to become too open, three very dark entities decided to attach themselves to me. Their arrival always brought forth a dark side of me. I would be surrounded by the scent of burnt charcoal and the musk of fear. I would shout out hateful comments, dark truths no one knew this person held.

These are also the ones who began to influence me to cut myself, pushing harder each time to cut deeper or longer. Me, being without anyone about talk to these things with, listened to them. Being already programed by the abuse that I was worthless, I believed their lies, as well. These episodes were labeled suicide attempts and also this is when I was mislabeled with many mental diagnoses. Perhaps my parents, and those counseling them, truly meant no harm. Unfortunately, what they did next only fed these dark entities a buffet of suffering.

Without someone to talk to, someone who would really listen and try to see past the medical and scientific jargon, the options were limited once the cutting became obvious. Hospitalization was declared as being required to keep me safe and to figure out how to 'help' me. This is the point of my story when Sean and I are doing lectures and presentations so many have their awakening. As hard as it is for me to speak about what is to follow, I know, from watching so many faces in the crowd, others need to hear it. Others need to know they aren't alone. So, I will tell it. Not for pity. Not for excuses. But for those who need to understand one simple thing in life – you are not alone.

Each time I arrived at the various mental institutions it was always the same greeting. A nurse, sometimes who was kind, sometimes who wasn't, would require me to be sedated and then take me to a room for seclusion and observation. I call this the appetizer course for the entities. They had me all to themselves. Even if I wanted to talk about it, no one would believe me at this point. One particularly horrible round I could feel them scratching into my skin, causing welts and raw, bloody lines along my legs and arms. The sounds of my screams brought one of those nurses. Of course, the nurse didn't believe it was being done by some dark force whispering to me. As far as the state was concerned, I was legally insane at this point and a threat to myself and others. Their answer to this spiritual abuse was to secure me to the bed to prevent myself from doing any further harm. This simple act left me to the mercy of not only the dark threesome, but also unable to escape the many spirits drawn to me who resided in the hospital. For six hours I was left to the screams of those begging for help, lost in their own pain, desperate to be heard and the three who came with me who continued to whisper to me words of hatred and taunting until the morning nurse arrived. By this time, I was empty of all hope, energy and the desire to live. This, for those in charge of my medical care, saw my state as a victory. My hysteria has passed. I was safe to be placed in a regular room.

The cutting was associated with the voices I heard. They were convinced if only I would stop listening to the voices, all of them, my behavior would return to the 'good girl' my family wanted me to be for them. The abuse was never brought up. In fact, the sexual abuse was blamed on the voices. The voices must have been telling me to take advantage of this adult in my life. I know they had a weakness for young girls and yet I didn't protect myself from them. So, I must have wanted the abuse due to the voices. One counselor even removed the word 'abuse' from our therapy because abuse doesn't happen to bad girls. I was a bad girl. I deserved it, but if I would only stop telling lies about the voices and admit I liked the sexual abuse I could be cured of my bad behaviors. Despite their best pep talks, the voices would not simply 'go away'. A new type of therapy was introduced.

Meals were always taken down in the cafeteria which was only for patients. For those who were progressing with their program correctly, there was one style of meal. For those of us who were not, there was another. The ones progressing often received meals of restaurant style quality. Including a dessert and soda as rewards. Which for a teen is pretty much the gold star of life. For those who were considered not progressing, they received a cold sandwich, a piece of fruit and water. Now by no means am I saying this was poor nutrition. Please don't confuse the statement. What this was, was a form of public humiliation, as a way to shame those who were not measuring up according to the medical team. Since our meal was much smaller than the others, we would often find ourselves sitting, watching the rest of the kids eating with our stomachs being loudly verbal with their complaints. Once again, it's our fault we were being bad children. All we had to do was comply with their medical advice to be good children and earn the rewards of good children.

Unfortunately, being good was not so simple for me. I could not simply just turn the voices off. Nor could I lie about it. For even when I tried, being in such a weakened state from constantly being tied to my bed, it would show upon my face. Now I was a bad girl and a disappointment. The very things the dark trio loved to whisper to me all night long. The medical team needed to find a different approach to reach past my refusal to follow my treatments. They did. The famous rubber band trick.

If you are not familiar with this technique, it is where one wears something upon which that can snap themselves with when a recurring bad habit or thought happens. The avoidance of the pain is thought to train someone to stop the behavior. I so desperately wanted to be this good girl they spoke of, wanted to go home to my family and make them love me, as the medical team said, I was willingly snapping my wrist with their large, thick rubber bands. They needed to be able to hear the sound of the act to know when to come over and speak with me about what caused the action so this was not your normal rubber band. I would confess each time what the voices said, who they belonged to, what the spirit wanted and each time I would be punished with additional snaps performed by the staff.  In a short amount of time, I was asked to wear long sleeves to hide the amount of bruising so that visitors would not ask questions. When my mother asked, she was assured this was all being done for my best interest and to trust the process. She did.

A male nurse, concerned the treatment plans weren't working, suggested a new technique. One which had been used long ago to cure patients with mental disorders.  He did warn it may hurt, but since it had gotten to the point my wrists were almost impossible to move from the pain, how much more damage could really be done? Fate has a way of answering that question in ways we wish she never thought of for us. He suggested I shock myself at night when the trio were at their worst. This would 'fry' that part of my brain, curing it, and allowing me to find peace from the voices and spirits I claimed to talk to all day and night. I was desperate. So, I did. For three nights, over and over again, I would stick the fork the nurse had stolen, and adjusted, from the cafeteria into sockets along the wall. I just wanted to find my normal. Whatever the costs.

This is often when someone will ask, "What about your Spirit Guides/ Guardian Angels/ Protectors? Why didn't they step in? Why didn't they help you?" They did. Or he did.

I have had one Spirit Guide my whole life. His name has changed as I have grown and worked with him but at the time, I had no training. I didn't know anything other than the voices and spirits were bad. To talk to them made me bad. I was doing the devil's work if I spoke with them. I didn't know I could have called out for help. I didn't know until the one I knew better than my own family came to me one night after several rounds of the fork in the socket. I remember it so vividly and I know that was my personal turning point in mediumship.

He came, leaning over my bed as I cried and told me, "We are going to go away for a little while. I'm going to take them all away, with me, until you call on us. Don't worry little witch, we will always be with you, listening, watching, and cheering for you, but right now, you need us to leave. We'll shut the door for you. You won't be able to hear us anymore, but you can write to us. Write to us, little witch, and we will gladly tell you all of our stories."

I watched, just as clear as if someone were to walk out the front door of your house, him ushering so many lights through the door. Some were bright white. Some were dark and blurry. Some even paused as if glancing at me one last time before they all faded into the glaring light behind the door. Then it was shut and the room, for the first time in my life, was silent. Completely still and in a weird way, I never felt more alone in my life than I did at that moment.

I was released from the hospital a few days later. A miracle. And I never returned to another one. To this day, I hate hospitals. I do my best to avoid them at all costs. I know, now deep in my heart and after many years of shadow work, the multiple hospitalizations were intended to help me and keep me away from my siblings and my abuser to prevent any secrets our house was hiding from coming into the light. I also know I had to go through that, survive that, so I might be here to tell you you're not alone. I gladly wear the scars of my childhood so that maybe others won't have to endure it. You. Are. Not. Alone.

If you take nothing from this chapter, take this, listen to your children. Listen to that deep part of you which knows your child better than any medical professional who has only interacted with them for a few moments. My mother knew something wasn't right with what they were labeling me, but she was unfortunately stuck in her own Hell dealing with the abuser and her own abuse from him. Do your research on labels given before declaring them. Does it fit? Truly?

Teens tend to pull away, hide their insecurities or cover them. So how are you as a parent supposed to know, to really investigate their private world without pushing them further away? You listen. Really listen. Let them know this is normal. They are normal. You see them. You accept them. You, most of all, believe them. These simple acts will let you decide on your own if the counselor is right, or if, just maybe, there is something spiritual happening with your child. Then, both of you, set a path to travel upon.

When he said to write about us, I didn't understand then what he was hinting at, what clues he was giving me to keep the door of my abilities cracked, waiting to be fully opened once again. In high school I would write these short stories about people, sometimes even horrific stories about their deaths and such situations. The stories won several awards of the arts and were genuinely loved by peers. I didn't know then, as I do now, this was how I was listening to them still. All I knew was writing helped with my emotions I would feel without any logical reason to be feeling a certain way about something or a place. It wasn't my emotions. It was spirits'. I kept notebooks after notebooks of these stories and poems. It was my release, I thought. When in fact, it was theirs. I didn't talk about the voices or the spirits or any of that anymore. I wrote it. He had shown me the way.

Most of my stories still are theirs. To this day I still pay homage to the spirits around me by telling their stories to people all over the world and these people never know it. Aimes, from *The Risen* series is a perfect example of this. Jedrek, from *The Great Hexpectations* series is modeled after my main Spirit Guide. There are many in the books who I interact with on a spiritual level in some way or another. It's my thanks to them and something we will talk about further in this book.

Encourage your teen to do the same. Talking about what they are seeing, or hearing, may be too much for them. It's not easy to admit to having this ability. Writing it though, that's their little world, a way to get it out of their heads without getting out into the world. It's how they can find their normal. After all, that's all they want right now – to feel normal.

The Witch I Am

Sometimes placing yourself in their shoes, writing as if you were them, is the easiest way to start your stories. Use their imagery, what they are telling you, to build the beginning of your work. Try present and past tense to see which feels better, easier, for them to speak with you. Feel no pressure to get it perfect. It's a story. A poem. Your normal. Make it yours.

## WRITING PROMPTS TO GET STARTED. GIVING SPIRITS A WAY TO COMMUNICATE:

1. I was _____ years old when I died.
2. I lived in a _____ in the town of _____.
3. My mother's name is _____.
4. My father's name was _____.
5. I looked like my siblings with our _____.
6. I didn't understand my death at first. It was so sudden when _____.
7. I wish I could have told my _____ at the time I knew they were there.
8. I wish I could tell _____, even now, how much I love them, how proud I was when _____.
9. I often times felt _____ but now in peace I feel only _____.

Once the story starts, or communication has been made, don't fear it. Let it just spill forth, never questioning what is being committed to paper. This is also called Automatic Writing. It's an amazing way to develop your mediumship, your communication with the other side, without any real risk to yourself.

Let your mind travel along with their life. Let your pen write without worry. As if listening to your favorite song and knowing the lyrics to write, you too will know their lyrics. It's their song. Just let them sing it to you.

If you're having trouble starting your writing process, it's most times due to fear. The fear of getting it right. The fear of is this me or them. The fear of letting go and allowing the spirits to 'speak' through you. We live so deep in our ego to survive that sometimes the hardest part about connecting to the other side is letting yourself let go, just be in the moment. Be present with nothing but this second. Don't focus on the facts or being right. Don't worry where the words are coming from. Trust in yourself and enjoy the activity. Every time you connect it builds the trust between yourself and spirit.

## AUTOMATIC WRITING

Find a spot where you will not be disturbed. This is your spot for the next few moments in time. No television. No loud music or people. No disruptions. Just you and an empty space somewhere near you for someone to join you in this space you have created.

Now, take a few deep breaths, letting the air fill you to such a degree there is no room for doubts, negativity, or fear. Expand your lungs with clean, healing air filling you with peace and comfort. When you feel yourself centered and rooted in this moment, invite someone to come sit with you. Maybe it's the voice you keep hearing randomly throughout the day. Maybe it's the spirit you have been seeing, waiting for you to acknowledge them. Maybe it's even your own spiritual team who has been trying to get in touch with you. Whoever, invite them to come join you without fear, but only trust with the understanding whoever is joining you is joining you with love.

At first you might just feel a slight change in the area. Maybe it's a temperature change. Maybe it's a smell or feeling. Let them know you are aware of them, and you would like to talk with them.

Start to move your hand, gliding the pen along the paper in either direction or even small circles. The motion isn't important. It's the action. When the words are ready, they will start to come forth. Trust what you are 'hearing'. Enjoy the conversation. When you feel the energy start to fade, thank them for visiting with you, wish them well, and allow them to step away.

This process may take some practice. Don't give up on it. Don't give up on yourself. I believe in you, and I believe you can do this!

*Use the next few pages to write.*

Marie F Crow

# The Witch I Am

Marie F Crow

The Witch I Am

I still draft these short stories to this day. I call them my Sunday Papers and each Sunday I will just sit down and write little blurbs about the spirits I have around me. Maybe these departed loved ones didn't get everything out at a gallery event or at the private appointment their family or friends held with me. Maybe at a paranormal investigation the spirits there didn't get a chance to step forward due to another spirit being more active for the investigators. Maybe a spirit noticed me while running errands and just wanted to talk to someone who can hear and see them. Either way, their stories, their message is being told and that's all most spirits want – to be heard and remembered. Don't be afraid to tell their stories. You, by healing yourself, are healing them. That's an amazing gift to give the world. You are an amazing gift to the world. What an honor it would be to meet you!

# Section Three – The Late Bloomers

*"Like wildflowers, you must allow yourself to grow in all the places people thought you never would."*
– E.V.

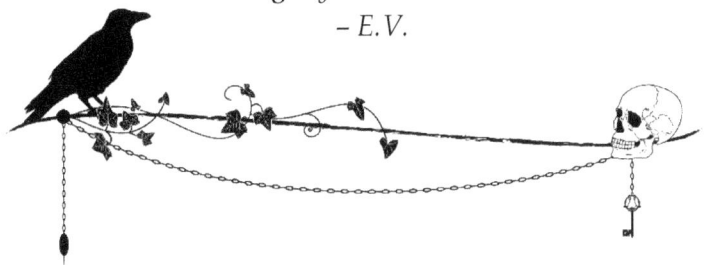

Just because you might not have been born with your abilities in full bloom doesn't mean life isn't just waiting for her perfect moment to kick your doors wide open. Remember how I mentioned sometimes our abilities decide to pop up when we find sudden trauma or shocking change in life? There are so many Sean and I have met who tell us after their divorce, or a loss of a loved one, or even a near death experience they began experiencing 'weird things', is often the quote. We are told over and over how they think they are 'going crazy' causing Sean and I to share a smile, invite them to sit down and have a conversation about what these 'weird things' exactly are that are happening to them.

They are often afraid to tell their friends or family for fear of being ridiculed, or mocked even, so they try to hide or ignore the changes that are happening around them. Unfortunately, spirits don't always understand our mortal issues. All they notice is that you notice them. You can sense them. And they are going to do their best to be sensed.

Items may start to go missing only to show up at some place you have already looked. Shadows may start appearing in the corner of your vision. You may start to feel as if you're not alone when in rooms that you are very much alone in. It's not uncommon to start picking up on people's emotions, or emotions which you can't explain because you know they aren't what you would normally feel.

This may become overwhelming. Of course, one would wonder if they were 'losing' their mind. Something which has never occurred before is now happening more and more often as you go about your life. On the one hand you are trying to heal from the recent change of events and on the other now you have all these unexplained things happening. It's a lot to deal with or understand if you have never experienced it before.

Perhaps you had abilities when you were younger and now, for some unknown reason, things which you thought were long go are back. Sean and I have heard plenty of cases where someone was able to see spirits as a child, but as life went on, the ability faded away. Sometimes spirits people knew well as a child have returned without an explanation, suddenly just being there in their life once again. Without someone to share this with, they shut down, fear it, ignore it and begin to worry over how to handle it. Luckily, or maybe unluckily, this is the largest group of those who attend our classes, seeking advice on what to do and how to handle it.

I remember after my divorce I found myself part of this group, too.

I learned from my childhood to never admit to things I knew or saw if I wanted to be accepted by certain members of my family. Even after 'being cured' they never really fully left. Shadow figures were always lurking. In fact, when *The Risen* series was first published, spreading so many spirits stories in the form of the zombies, and the characters, our house seemed to become very crowded. My ex-husband would often joke about the shadow figure who suddenly became a part of our lives. Our family knew not to go downstairs at night without announcing our arrival. Otherwise, this figure would be waiting to startle us with his presence or by slamming doors as we walked past them. As more books began to be published, more spirits moved in. We even had one who looked exactly like our youngest daughter I named Lilly in the novels. There were times when my ex-husband and I would dare the other to go check and be sure the little girl we just saw running through the house at night was the spirit or if our youngest was playing a prank on us. In fact, when our youngest daughter learned how to crab walk upside down like the girl in *The Exorcist,* she thought it was very amusing to run at her father and I to watch our reaction since she was aware of the spirit. It was at this point I would remind her I was an author of zombie novels and knew to aim for the head when scared. It never helped the situation when someone would bring to the conversation the fact that almost every zombie movie begins with a blonde little girl attacking someone.

After the divorce, the shadow figures, the quick flashes of spirits evolved quickly.

Almost overnight I went from a stable life to sleeping on my own front porch, to living out of my car, bouncing from houses until I finally was able to move into my own apartment. The remorse of a failed marriage, the adjustments my daughters were struggling with, the guilt members of my family were placing upon me stirred all the old whispers once chanted to me as a child. I began cutting again and one night, the act of letting the pain out almost cost me my life.

When I needed my family the most, just as when I was a little girl, they were slowly turning away from me. In fighting to find myself by announcing not only was I divorcing, but also turning away from religion and embracing spirituality, I was denounced and even had death threats placed upon me should certain family members ever see me. I was alone, and honestly if it wasn't for Sean, I would not have been strong enough to survive for my daughters.

There's a moment before death when you are in the in-between, not crossed over, but not a part of this world either. It's here where one might see their own body or interact with departed loved ones in the bright light people often speak of with near death experiences. For me, in my in-between, was the man I remembered from that day in the hospital. He was leaning against a wall, shaking his head with amusement. Around him were people I have never met, women from my mother's family line, smiling at me as if we were the best of friends. Oddly, I had no knowledge of them.

He explained to me these were women just like me. Women from my line who could also see the dead, interact with the dead and control the dead. He used the word witch because it's the most common explanation mankind has placed upon those like us. When they hugged me, it felt as if peace was an embrace. Everything I had refused to admit to, believe in or trust was handed to me yet again. Like a key to a lock, their love and acceptance opened knowledge I didn't know I held inside of me.

"Are you ready to head back my little witch?" he had asked me.

Sensing my fear, one of the ladies whispered to me to never let the ones of our blood worry me. Those who have forgotten would be reminded when they met once again. I remember her mischievous wink. I held it as if it were a security blanket every time my heart broke under that member of my family's hatred. That night also taught me no matter how far my family walked from me, my family walks with me.

Upon my return to this world, the door he had left with but a crack was now a swinging gate. The dead came and went as they willed. I wasn't writing at this point in my life. I had no way to deal with their arrival discreetly. With Sean's help, the help of trusted friends and the woman I call my pagan wife, Leslie, I learned how to not only accept what I am, who I am, but also how to talk about it without fear.

But it wasn't such a simple thing. I was determined to prove what I was seeing, feeling and doing was real to those who mocked and doubted me. This meant I had to truly dive into this new me, learning how to control my abilities not just accept them. Of course, there were many blunders along the way which we still all laugh about to this day.

Our favorite was the manipulation of electricity. My moods would affect lights, radios and televisions. On more than one occasion Leslie and or Sean would tell me to chill for fear of blowing light bulbs around me. Sean would have to ask me what is wrong when the television would change channels or have the picture distorted. Our running joke was often strangers making comments about how the electronics never behaved the way they were when I was around, not understanding no matter how many times they adjusted it or flat out hit whatever was distorted it would not fix it. How I wasn't outed more times than I was is amazing.

I took class after class to learn how to turn the fleeting pictures in my mind into full conversations with the dead. Earning certification after certification as if that would somehow gain the approval of the family who mocked me. A path started for preservation became my salvation.

I learned how to become a true trance medium, allowing the dead to enter my body and speak for themselves. I discovered the ability to alter electricity so I could use it to communicate with those who have passed in haunted locations and during seances. The voices I once defined as evil now heal those they have left behind with final parting words and messages. I might have never gained the love I craved but I have learned to love the life I now live without those who abandoned me.

There are still times where I have to remind myself of who I am. Mediumship isn't a science and there are always those who mock it. There are times I wonder if it would be easier to force the door shut once again and live a life without my invisible friends which have rejoined me. But just like those who have once again been reunited with gifts and abilities, or those who have just discovered them, these things are a part of us. It's what makes us who we are and helping so many embrace this part of their lives is more rewarding than any certification I have earned. There's a peace to living fully in your soul. Why should we allow anyone to rob us of that?

The most important thing you must remember about your journey, because this is a journey, is it's your journey. You don't have to answer to anyone about it. That is a very freeing thought. It's also a very scary one because most of us have never made our truths a priority for fear of upsetting someone else in some fashion. Growing in a way people don't understand will always upset them.

Whichever path you take, choice you make, or bridge you might have to burn, it's all done by you because this is not a journey one can take for you, but merely with you, as you discover the strength to become who you truly wish to be in this life.

Never let anyone who is not walking with you fill you with doubts over what you know to be true. Ever. Those who laugh at you, mock you and disappoint you, understand this is not their journey. You may find your path to discover your abilities taking you further and further away from these people. Let it. As painful as it might be, let it.

This moment, this life you are making, is yours. What an amazing journey it will be when you take that first step into forever, into your soul space where you are meant to live. The peace you will find surrounded in your own love and acceptance is warmer than any love someone might offer you. Because it's yours and no one can take it away from you ever again.

## *YOUR HEART SPACE*

To find the confidence to embark upon this journey let's work on your heart space.

Your heart space is the part of your spirit where you live in love and joy. It's where your purpose comes from and is normally an instant way to calm fears and doubts.

Lifting your vibration is easiest done from this space.

I want you to find a comfortable position to sit in.

In a pattern of three to five breaths, breathe in for four seconds, hold for seven seconds and then exhale for eight seconds. Let the burdens of your day slip away with each exhale.

Placing your right hand over your heart, continue your breathing pattern but now feel the pattern under your hand. You might not feel anything at first. As you sit, repeating your breathing pattern, the beat of your heart will slowly be felt, growing stronger under your fingers.

You are now in your heart space. You are connected to your heart and your subconscious mind.

Once you enter this space, repeat to yourself how strong you are. Remind yourself this is your journey, and you deserve to explore it despite what others might say about it. Remind yourself you are an amazing person, a beautiful soul. Tell yourself all the positive things about your life while sitting in this healing space. Let your words slip into your heart and your subconscious mind removing negativity and fears which are holding you down.

As your words fill your heart feel the glow spreading from your chest until it covers your whole body.

You are fully encased in love allowing you to have the courage to face any negativity.

To close the session, take one last full deep breath, exhaling slowly, asking your spiritual team to be with you as you need them.

****

The Heart Space meditation is a simple tool to have in your spiritual toolbox. It's a good foundation to the other meditations we will add in other sections. The difference with this meditation is it is built for you boosting your energy. Whereas other meditations are designed to help you lift your energy to connect with the other side, or spirit. The first step should always be raising your energy before trying to raise your energy for communication. You must be of good heart and mind to receive clear, evidential mediumship messages. If unable to do the heart space meditation, remember, music has always been used to lift the 'spirit' of a ceremony before worship may begin. You, too, can simply find your favorite music to empower yourself before sitting for divination.

# Section Four – Your Spiritual Team

*"The spiritual journey is the unlearning
of fear and the acceptance of love."
– Marianne Williamson*

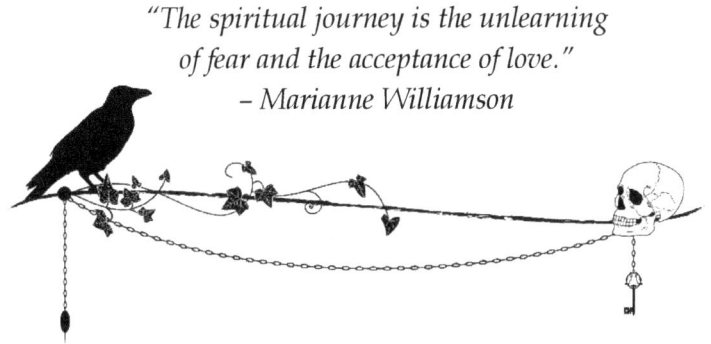

I talk about my spiritual team often. It's not to preach about their importance or try to enforce the need to have one upon others. I talk about them because they have saved my life, in one way or another, many times. My guides have been with me when many were not. Unfortunately, it took me too many years before I realized how valuable they are to a solid spiritual life. From saving me from the abuse, to ushering the spirits away to keep me safe, to whispering clues about life, my team has been there.

Being a trance medium from an early age without my team in place there were many times spirits were able to slip in and out of my body when I was not in full control. One of Sean's most traumatic memories is the night I had to be physically restrained while a spirit was able to take control of me. This spirit was so hateful with the things it said that Sean still has emotional wounds from that night. Of course, then we had no friends in this field, no one to call for help. There aren't many books about what to do when your fiancée suddenly comes under spiritual attack. It was several hours of Sean and two of our close friends waiting it out until I was able to come back to myself.

Needless to say, if I had the understanding of my team's provided protection as I do now, this could have been avoided. It took some time and training before Sean felt comfortable leading our trance mediumship sessions. It was Leslie who initially entered into the training with me and then gradually handed the reins to Sean. Sean's reluctance to be involved in trance mediumship is why we believe the spirit of an older woman named Bridget loves to pick on him when she comes through. To be fair, if you attend one of our events Bridget will most likely pick on you, too.

After that night I took every class, bought every book, and talked to every 'expert' about Spirit Guides, Deities, and ancestors. I learned how to slip into their world through self-hypnosis and meditation. I discovered how to access my past lives to revisit lessons I have already lived through with hopes to avoid the same mistakes. Most importantly, I learned how to call my team to me in this realm whenever I needed them. I invite them to walk with me openly, every day, allowing me to hear their chatter about my life, as well as those I come in contact with through a client or just in every day passing. I also invoke my ancestors before any activity involving the craft as their knowledge often aids me in my work. It is the ladies we spoke of earlier who helped me understand the finer workings of the craft. I listen to their advice without any hesitation, and I talk of them often during classes I teach or upon the podcast I hold every Sunday.

I call this my SB7 mode of life, walking in free, open communication every day. In other words, my head space is filled, and used to communicate, with the beyond through the same theory as radio stations an SB7 would use to facilitate dialog with the dead. From my main male Guide, to my spiritual team, even the dead who try to test my boundaries, will speak to me. Sometimes it's just little blips, random chatter or sounds to allow me to associate them to the person in front of me. Sometimes it's what I call the peanut gallery as my main Guides chime in during classes about what topics to be sure I cover for those attending. Most of my classes are channeled due to this for any lesson plan I put together, he overrides during the class. Now I just make bullets points and hope he stays on track.

In fact, the dead with me are often those belonging to my closest friends. This group loves to gather around me, often just sitting in the room I am in or clamoring around my house as if they have made themselves at home. From topless ancestors riding horses to shout about their hatred for a patriarchy, to grandmothers drinking tea while judging those who enter the shop, departed fathers and roller-skating nuns, I have them all.

The most important member of my team is my guardian animal, or spirit animal. It is he who guides me under when we do trance, and it is he who watches spiritually over me to protect my energy while performing trance healing. In this realm, he will show his glowing eyes when a client makes him uneasy or when someone enters my space who should not be there. He often sits at the side of me during our gallery events, walking beside me to be sure I am spiritually protected during the two to three hour shows. In fact, if you watch close, you will notice me walking around a space as if I am trying to avoid something. It's him. Just like my dogs at home, my spirit animal also loves to somehow always end up underfoot, waiting for the perfect opportunity to dart through and trip me. It's amusing until I let Sean pick the outfit for the night and the short skirt threatens to show more than the crowd paid for as I stumble.

Discovering how to communicate with your Spirit Guide does not have to be the long endurance of trials as mine turned out. Your Guides are waiting for you. They came down to this realm with the single purpose of being with you in this lifetime. Chances are you are already aware of them. Now, we just have to allow you to understand their forms of communication so when they are reaching out you will understand their message.

Please understand, once you start opening doorways to the other side, your beacon of mediumship will become brighter and brighter, attracting more spirits to try to speak with you. Things will start to move quickly as you explore the veil separating us from the other side. For some, this will be terrifying. These are the ones who will refuse to continue any further. For some, this is thrilling. It confirms everything they have been feeling in their lives. They will push further to explore and test their abilities. Whichever group you belong to, I encourage you to at least try to connect with your spiritual team if no other reason than to have that connection with the Divine. This connection will empower you in ways that words cannot be put into picture. You will have an inner fire. This fire which will burn and warm you with confidence because you know, despite what those around you or even the world might tell you, you are, in fact, loved.

You are protected and cared for by a power no human may take from you. You have a supportive source when you feel alone. They are always there, waiting on you to reach for them so they may look to comfort you, guide you, and love you.

They have known you since birth and don't judge your mistakes or that part of yourself you hate. To them, you are perfect because you are perfect. You are perfectly human, and we are all filled with mistakes and things we hate about ourselves.

## CALLING UPON THE GUIDES

There are several meditations one can use to settle into a relaxed space to spiritually travel to meet their Guides. Whereas this may sound scary, I promise you there is no risk other than possibly falling asleep from entering such a deep state of relaxation. Read through the meditations and then pick the one which feels the best for your energy. Or try them all and enjoy the unique styles of communication.

## THE GRAND TREE

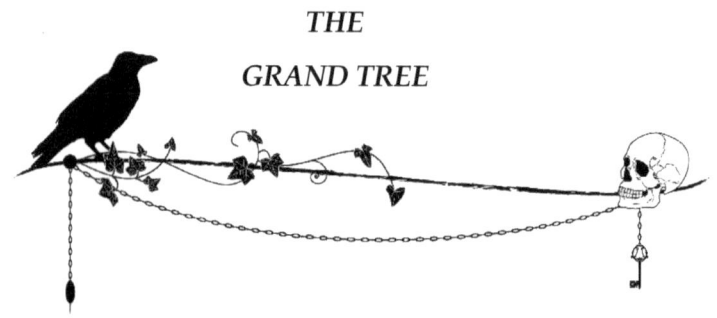

I want you to start by entering your heart space we mentioned earlier. Let your mind and body become one with your breathing exercise. Allow yourself to fully slip into the loving energy surrounding you with the sensation of peace and tranquility, knowing you are safe to let go of the day-to-day worries in this moment of time. This is your time. Your spiritual moment to heal and refuel.

Once you reach this state, close your eyes and feel yourself start to drift away. I want you to picture a long pathway through tall, green trees. Stand here for a moment, breathing in the fresh air scented with your favorite flowers blooming all around you. You are eager to walk along this path, eager to discover what awaits you inside the forest.

As you travel along the winding curves take notice of everything around you. Tell yourself you will remember these details when you awaken.

Going deeper and deeper into the forest you discover a tall tree standing by itself in the center of a clearing. This tree has a door at its base. It seems to beckon you towards it. While walking towards it you feel as if you've been here before. You are at ease, without any worries as you enter through this door.

Through this door is your personal spiritual refuge. It's your spiritual home. Every inch of it is designed as you would design such a refuge. Take note of everything mentally to remember when you awaken.

Once you are familiar with your new space, pay attention to the pictures upon the walls. These are the pictures of your Spirit Guides. Try to take notice of these pictures. How many are hanging along this wall? Can you see any faces? Any aspects of them? How do you feel as you stare at these pictures?

Next, I want you to sit in a chair located inside this refuge. While sitting in this chair, envision a ray of sunshine coming through the top of the tree to surround you with its warmth. This bright, yellow ray of light fills you with spiritual energy as it shines through your crown chakra. Once your crown chakra is filled with energy, fill this light flowing to your third eye, opening it to the spiritual world around you. It then flows to your throat chakra so you may speak with your guides. Allow the light to travel to each chakra opening and preparing it to sense the spiritual energy all around you.

When you feel fully recharged, stand, and leave this place knowing you can return at any time. This is your personal spiritual refuge. Your sacred space when feeling disconnected and needing to recharge.

As you leave your tree, take notice of how tall its branches are, connecting it to the Divine energy all around it. See how the roots run deep and thick into the ground, securing it with grounding energy of safety.

Travel the path back to where you began, bringing you out of your meditative state. Sit for a moment, moving your toes, rolling your neck, and gently stretching to reconnect your mind space with your body.

*Before you end this session, take a moment and write down everything you noticed during your meditation.*

Marie F Crow

1. What was the path made of?

2. Where there any obstacles along the way?

3. What flowers were blooming? Why those flowers?

4. How did your tree look? How did the inside appear?

5. Were you able to see the faces in the frames? What do you remember about them?

6. How did the ray of sunshine feel? Do you notice any differences in how you are feeling now verses before the meditation?

Try this meditation often when working on your spiritual connection. You will notice that things change each time you visit your refuge. This space will reflect how your spiritual energy currently is upon entering it. Use this not only as a way to further your communication but also to self-check your progress. Compare your notes each time to keep track of these changes.

Be mindful of the pictures on the wall, as well. Spirit Guides come and go as we evolve. You might notice new frames or less frames from time to time when you visit. This is perfectly normal. In fact, it might be the same if you choose to add an ancestor wall to your refuge. Just like Spirit Guides, when we have learned all we can from our ancestors they, too, will pass back to the source of energy some call Heaven and others simply refer to as the Divine Source. Either way, this can warn us about new spiritual lessons we are about to embark upon, or even lessons we have finally mastered as the number of frames either grow or shrink upon the walls.

This little treehouse of yours can be more than just a place to refuel, but also a way of gathering clues about what's ahead for you in your journey if you pay close enough attention to it.

## STROLL IN THE PARK

For this meditation start with three to five deep, slow inhales and exhales. Focus on each part of your body, tensing and then releasing it to allow your body to rid itself of the day's tension. Start with your toes moving up your body until you reach your head, tensing each section for a few seconds before releasing your muscles. If any areas still feel tight, revisit them, holding them longer before releasing their tension asking yourself why this part is still tense. Is it associated with a chakra? A memory? Or something as simple as a difficult day at the gym? Either way, take a moment to evaluate it to be sure your team isn't already giving you clues about what's to come.

Once your body is fully relaxed, go ahead and close your eyes. Continue with deep breathing until you start to feel a state of deep relaxation and floating away from your body.

As you start to drift, I want you to picture a perfect park bench amid a field. See the grass as you cross this field to reach the bench. Breathe deeply of the clean air, relaxing further as the many scents pull you deeper into this sacred space of yours.

Have a seat on your bench, sitting comfortably as if you've been to this field many times. As you sit there, you notice a person is walking towards you. Slowly, this person comes into focus before you, joining you on the bench.

You feel no alarm or discomfort with this person. This person feels like an old friend you haven't talked to in a long time. Introduce yourself and have them do the same. Make a note to remember everything about this person from how they smell, look, sound and even how they make you feel when they are near you.

Talk to this person now. Tell them about your day, your goals, where you want your life to go just as you would with a friend as the two of you catch up. Ask this new friend for any advice they might have concerning the problems you are sharing with them. When the conversation comes to an end, thank this new friend using their name. Let them know you are looking forward to returning to speak with them. Watch as this person leaves you alone to sit for a moment more to enjoy the peace of this location before you leave.

When you are ready, stand from the bench and walk away from the field mentally awakening and returning to a fully aware state. Before you move, take a moment to stretch, making sure you are fully back and completely aware of your surroundings.

*Before you end this session, take a moment and write down everything you noticed during your meditation.*

1. How did this meditation feel?

2. Are there any things you took notice of in the field while waiting for your Spirit Guide to arrive?

3. Were you able to connect with the person who visited you? How did that feel?

4. What was the name your Spirit Guide gave you? Have you heard this name before? If so, where? If you did not receive a name, how did their energy feel when in their presence? Have you felt it before? When and where?

5. What advice did you receive about your situation?

6. Do you notice any difference in how you feel now than how you felt before entering the meditation?

## WHO WILL GUARD ME

To meet your spirit animal is remarkably similar to meeting your guides. Ironically, you may find you have always been aware of your spirit animal due to collecting a certain animal without any reason behind it. This is often the case after we do this meditation. Students come awake with a shock because they have a whole collection of a certain animal they started when they were young, or we hear how a student has always loved this animal their whole life. Spirit is always working behind the scenes in our life to let their presence be known.

Find a comfortable spot to sit or lay down as to your preference. Focus on slowing your breath, inhaling deeper each time and exhaling slower, as well. With each exhale, imagine you are slowly drifting away, freeing yourself from the stress of the day.

As you drift away let your mind hear the sounds of a forest. Hear the leaves moving in the wind. Hear the birds singing their songs to one another. Focus on hearing these sounds until you can picture this forest before you.

Walk through this forest until you find a spot to sit. Take in all that surrounds you. Be part of this forest. Let the sounds and feeling of the ground underneath you bring you comfort and peace, allowing you to slip further into this space and further away from your body and the concerns life holds for you.

As you sit, ask your spirit animal to come to you. This may take a moment. Don't worry if you find yourself sitting for some time until they make their arrival.

When your animal spirit shows itself, greet it. Ask for its name. Ask how it will help you in this life.

Spend time together getting used to how it feels to be around your spirit animal. This is the sensation you will be looking for when you are living your spiritual life and working with spirit.

Ask your spirit animal how you will know when they are around you when not in the spiritual realm.

After you have spent the desired time with your spirit animal thank them for making their presence known today.

Stand and begin to exit the forest as you mentally become awake and back fully aware of your surroundings. Take a moment to stretch to be sure you are fully awake before making any sudden movements.

*Before you end this session, take a moment and write down everything you noticed during your meditation.*

# The Witch I Am

1. What sounds pulled you to the forest?

2. What was the forest like once you fully arrived at the location?

3. Did you notice anything particular about the forest while waiting for your spirit animal?

4. What is your spirit animal?

5. How did it feel when your spirit animal came to you?

6. Have you felt these sensations before?

7. Were you able to gain a name from your spirit animal this session?

8. How will they let you be aware of them when they are around you?

9. Do you feel any different now than before you started the meditation?

# NICE TO MEET YOU

For those who find deep meditation difficult, there is a lighter form of meditation one can use to discover their guides. We often start our classes with this one because of how simple and yet effective it is for connecting to the other side. It is also very versatile. This light meditation can be used to communicate with anyone, not just your Spirit Guides. If you wish to speak to an ancestor or Deity, follow the same steps just replacing the name of who you are requesting to meet. Let's begin.

I want you to find a space you will not be disturbed, a space you feel comfortable in and very familiar with what is inside of it; a place you already use to seek to find peace and calming but preferably not your bedroom unless you prefer lucid dreaming as your form of communication.

Take a few deep breaths filling your lungs deeply so that your whole chest lifts from using your diaphragm. Exhale these breaths slowly, letting the air roll from your body with no rush. Each time you inhale I want you to feel the clean air filling you and with each exhale you are letting go of any negativity of the day your body is holding. Do this as many times as needed until you reach a state of relaxation.

As you sit in the new state of peace, I want you to mentally ask for your Spirit Guide to come a step closer to you.

Take notice of any sensations you are feeling as they step forward.

Now, ask them to step away.

Take notice of how it feels when they are not near you.

Once again, ask them to step close.

Does it feel the same?

With your guide standing close to you, ask them to gently touch you, showing you how they will let you know when they are around and need your attention.

Sit for a moment with this new sensation, becoming familiar with it.

Ask your guide for their name as they are touching you, allowing the connection to be stronger than before when they were just standing beside you.

Repeat this process as many times as you like to fully become aware and understand the feelings of their presence in your space. They don't mind. Trust me. They want you aware of them, too.

Thank your Spirit Guide for coming forward today before you open your eyes and return to a fully awake stage.

*Before you end this session, take a moment and write down everything you noticed during your meditation.*

1. How did it feel when your guide stepped forward?

2. How did it feel when your guide stepped away?

3. Did you notice anything else when your guide was close, such a scent or feeling?

4. Which side did you guide step close to?

5. Was it the same side of your body each time?

6. Where did your guide touch you as your sign they are with you?

7. How did it make you feel to be touched by your guide?

8. Did you hear a name during this session?

9. Have you ever felt these sensations before now?

10. Do you notice any differences in how you are feeling now verses how you felt before the mediation?

___

Try these meditations several times before giving up on the situation. You may not have gotten all the information you wanted to the first time. Despite your guides being here with the purpose to help you in this life, it does take time to build the connection with them.

There is nothing wrong with it progressing slowly. It is not a reflection of you, or your abilities, or your ability to connect. Be kind to yourself as you start to move into the spiritual world. We all progress at various levels and you will progress at the level which is perfect for you.

Progressing too fast can trigger health issues as your body is a regulation of energy. From migraines to physical exhaustion, pushing your body to constantly raise its vibrations will have impacts upon it. Athletes don't start at the Olympics. They train until their bodies can, and will, perform at the level of healthy expectations of their sport. You, right now, are learning to become a spiritual athlete. Take the time to train before tossing in the towel. Respect your body's boundaries and in time you too will be able to reach your goals with your craft.

# Section Five – Leaning into Your New Life

*"Once you've started down that road to
self-discovery, no matter how treacherous
the before you, you can't turn back. The
universe doesn't allow it."*
– Lisa Unger

I would love to tell you this new aspect of your life will be rainbows and songbirds. I wish I could, but I won't. You are about to face struggles most will never encounter. You will also face moments of great healing most will never be blessed to discover. Even if you never openly admit to these amazing gifts you are given, just simply acknowledging the many lost souls wandering right beyond sight for most will give comfort to those souls. Imagine hurting, being confused and lost. Everyone around you is ignoring you. Now, out of nowhere, someone not only sees you, but tells you it's okay. You're okay. I'm listening to you. Please, tell me of your suffering. How breathtaking and healing would this be for this spirit?

That's now you. You are now healing those who many cannot. You are breathtaking.

It won't always be easy. There will be times when your spiritual connection will be weak, if not completely silent, leaving you wondering and filled with doubts. The dark voices, which always play in the hidden corners of our minds, will become loud enough to fill that void where once confidence in yourself lived.

You might even find yourself tempted to listen to them as they echo all the negative opinions people threw your way when you started this journey, like heavy rocks against your soul. It's in this space of time that your spiritual team may test you. Are you strong enough to listen to their whispers encouraging you to reach the next level of your path? Or will you cave when it gets too hard because of the deafening critics? Especially when that critic is you.

Understand that even in our most broken state, your spiritual team will never leave you. Even when their voices and their presence feel so extremely far away, they are still with you. They will always be with you. The question is – will you do the demanding work to recover the link, or let the critics win?

There are times I become lazy, overwhelmed with life and her responsibilities, I let my responsibilities as a medium and witch slip. I lose focus with the dead, or worse, become overburdened with them because I have allowed my boundaries to fail. This failure of boundaries can lead to physical symptoms such as brain fog, difficulty concentrating, depression, anxiety, lack of appetite, fatigue, and agitation to name just a few. Sean will be the first to point it out, asking me when was the last time that I worked with my team. This is pretty much his way of telling me to go eat a spiritual snickers and fix my attitude.

Sean has become so attuned to my changes he often knows when a spirit is around me before even I do by how I am acting. He will sigh and ask, "Who is talking to you?". It catches me by surprise because I fight not to show someone is around but, in my attempt, to hide it, I was making it rather obvious.

You might have similar situations where your friends or family ask you if you're okay or if you are listening to them because you are trying so hard to not listen to the other side you are actually not listening, or present, with either side. You've lost your focus on how to control the divide. You aren't reaching through the veil between our two worlds. You are stuck in the veil fighting to reach through to either side. Whereas some mediums prefer to live and walk fully connected with both sides, most mediums who are not full-time mediums, and even those who are, do not find this a comfortable way to live. That choice is up to you.

I, personally, live fully open, but with boundaries. Which is why I must always do my best to live fully in spiritual peace and in connection with my team. Neglecting the needs of your body and your mental space will cause your protection link to be weakened. Just as when you're in an emotional dark place and those spirits who thrive on that pain will take advantage of that weakened state, even the sincerest spirits can overstep boundaries when the link to your team is weakened. This is how attachments form. Despite what Hollywood would like to present, there are no positive attachments.

Once your abilities start to grow, so will the number of spirits who are drawn to you. There are many ways to help set, enforce, and embrace your spiritual boundaries and protection. I'll include a few of the exercises I use with students to bolster their abilities or to simply activate them. Please understand some of these will need regular practice, but in time, your connections will improve.

## *OPEN FOR COMMUNICATION – SETTING BOUNDARIES*

In the beginning of reaching out to speak with the dead, your Spirit Guides, or even just your ancestors, you will need to not only set your boundaries with them, but also start letting your subconscious mind understand your boundaries. Up until now your subconscious mind has been the operating system which has been running your life. We need to find a way for you to work with both. Basically, we need to let you and the dead know when you are open for communication.

## EXERCISE ONE - THE BOX

It's not surprising those of us in divination and the craft seem to have various wooden boxes everywhere. They hold our cards, our crystals, or herbs and so much more. There is almost something electric when we open these boxes. Our minds know the beloved trinkets and items secreted away inside of them just waiting to be allowed to play. We can use this same excitement for spirits, too.

First, we must pick out the perfect box to hold our tools. These tools are whatever you feel comfortable with and can change, or even evolve, through your journey. Make sure you pick a box large enough!

Set aside time each night to be open for communication. Just as when you call a friend, make sure you have a spot where you will not be disturbed. Once ready, let the dead, or your spiritual team know you are about to open the box. Select the tool of divination you will be using during this session. Invite spirit to step forward to speak with you, leaving the box open while holding your communication. Think of the box as a doorway to the other side. While it is open, you are available.

When you are through with this session, thank the spirit you have been communicating with before placing the tool of divination back into the box. As you close this new favorite box of yours let the spirits know you are no longer willing to speak with them. They will simply have to wait until you are once again open for communication.

This exercise, while seemingly simple, allows you to start setting boundaries for yourself and the understanding of how to control your abilities. When you set the rules early in your development you set yourself on a firm foundation of trust with yourself, your spiritual team and those who are wanting to speak with you.

I personally, to this day, keep my tarot cards, bones and witch's runes in a box. As described above, the other side knows when this box is opened, they may step forward to communicate with the client sitting in front of me. This has allowed boundaries for me and for the departed who are eagerly waiting for their family and friends to arrive for their appointment. Only my team, my personal dead and the dead of those who are closest to me are allowed open communication with me. The rest, for the sake of my sanity and energy, must wait their turn. I suggest you do the same if this is how you wish to start.

Should you find a spirit trying to communicate with you outside of this practice, simply remind them you are only open for communication when you signal them, when you open the box. You would not allow someone to simply walk in and disturb you while at work or in the middle of your day. Don't allow spirits to, either. If they wish to work with you, let it be known, your boundaries must be respected.

## CHARMS AND JEWELRY

Did you know that many witches and mediums will wear certain crystals for protection? We also wear them to enhance our gifts. Rings, bracelets and sometimes even necklaces are rich with symbolism. Some of these symbols are obvious. Sometimes only the one wearing the piece knows what the intricate metal work is or the crystal's use. It is their personal charm made, or selected, for them.

Much as when you open the box, placing these items upon your body signals the other side you are open for communication. It does not have to be fancy or shiny. It does not matter if it's gold or silver. All that matters is when you hold this item in your hands you feel confident to listen to the energy around you.

There are several different ways to allow the item to serve this purpose for you.

After finding your statement piece, the piece of jewelry which just fits, you may meditate with it. Envision in your mind during this meditation you are wearing this item while evolving your abilities with confidence. See yourself standing proud and safe while wearing it. Imagine how amazing it feels when wearing this item allowing you to be confident in the messages you are receiving. Set your boundaries with this item, as well. Concentrate on how your abilities will work when it is worn and how they won't when the item is off. This item is like a light switch for you. After your meditation, wear it and practice your divination. Please remember to keep this item in a safe space from you when you are not open for communication.

Find jewelry which relates to your divinity or something with a symbol that resonates with you. Many wear keys as a link between the doors to our world and theirs. When the skeleton keys are worn it symbolically represents the opening of any doorway. The sound of the keys clanging together dispels energy almost pushing a ceremonial feel around you of protection. Skeleton keys are also sometimes placed on tables before seances, once again allowing the doors to be unlocked. When the keys are tucked away, the doors cannot be opened, preventing being opened for communication.

There are herbs in the craft which are understood to help facilitate communication, or reaching between the veil such as thyme, allspice, myrrh, mugwort, wormwood, frankincense, dandelion, and tobacco are some of the most common, but feel free to experiment. Once you have selected your herbs, grind them to a powder to place in a bowl which will also be used to store this mixture. I always add graveyard dirt to my bowl, stirring it together. In this bowl, I place my jewelry I use to help open the veil, and allow me to feel confident while doing paranormal work. I invite you to do the same. This will keep the jewelry charged, cleared and ready to work with you due to the energy of the herbs and dirt. This is also sometimes called root work and will be covered in another book.

Find a link to the other side. Do you have a piece of jewelry from a special family member? A ring from your grandmother? Earrings from an aunt? A necklace your mother would always wear? Perhaps something from your father? This item is already infused with your ancestor's energy. Would this family member have allowed any harm to come to you? Was this member always loving and supportive, healing you in your moments of life when you needed them? Do you just feel closer to them when you wear it? Chances are, they too feel close to you when you wear it. Wear this item when you want to speak with them or have them speak with spirits for you. When I know I am going to go to a location which might have questionable energy, I always wear a necklace of my mother's. I know she will keep me safe, allowing me to feel confident despite the activity of the location.

These are just a few ways to attune your items to work with you. Perhaps your spiritual practice has its own way. Feel free to try several of these. Pick the ones which work best for you. Never worry about what works best for another. Remember, this is your journey and you're trying to discover what works best to help you connect.

There might also come times when your tried-and-true methods no longer work, or don't feel as strong as they once did to aid you. This could mean you have evolved in your journey and are being asked to dive deeper into your practice. Be prepared for new spiritual lessons during this time, or as often called, bumps in the road. Remember though, your team or Deity will never bring something to you they aren't willing to help you get through. Sometimes the lesson isn't in the passing, but how you handled the bumps during it.

# Section Six – Now What?

*"Courage starts with showing up and
letting ourselves been seen."*
– Brene Brown

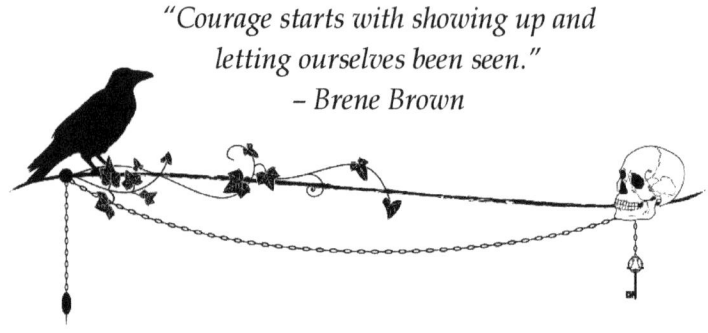

Through this journey we have talked about how to help our children, our teens, and even yourself if you find new experiences you might remember or new experiences you want answers for or feel drawn towards. As stated, it's not uncommon as we age to feel the tug to explore a part of ourselves we have always been afraid to label, accept, or even speak about for fear others might not understand. We deny ourselves a piece of ourselves, fighting to limit ourselves to be sure others feel comfortable in our presence. No one is more in your presence than you are. This is why, no matter what the subject is, it is so especially important to feel comfortable, and love yourself. I often tell people it is none of my business what others think of me. All that matters is what I think of me, because there will be times when I am all I will have to get myself through situations which life may throw at me.

This is not to say I am not guilty of being a people pleaser at times. I am very guilty of it. Guilty to the degree I often have to self-examine situations to gut check if the situation is healthy for me, or harmful, as I continue to limit myself for someone else's benefit. Every time you do this, you are diminishing your own light, your vibrations, your self-confidence. I encourage you to start, right now, to never dim your light.

## The Witch I Am

You were given this light for a reason. Perhaps the reason is yet to have been discovered, but there is a reason. If you were to give up before this discovery what an injustice you have done to yourself and the world who is waiting for your gifts.

You must keep yourself grounded from ego. This is also something I sometimes stumble upon so please don't think I am lecturing. We are human. It is a natural urge to want to be as good, if not better, than others sometimes. This desire to be seen and acknowledged, after all, is what might have led us to our open abilities. So, let's not hate ourselves for it.

There will always be someone better than the next in all aspects of life. This is not meant to be a competition, but a collective. Strengths and weaknesses are what make strong bonds among friends as well as those of us walking this path. Find those who are also trying to grow into their abilities. One, this will allow you to have those in your life who understand what you might be going through. Two, you will find those who can show you how to grow without fear of judgment.

Most metaphysical stores hold mediumship circles, or should know where one might be found. Mediumship circles are normally groups who gather several times a month, to once a month, to allow the members to practice upon one another. Since these are normally not friends of your everyday life, or family members, you can trust what you are reading from these people are not due to you just talking about a situation earlier in the week. Most times, you know nothing about them, providing you with a blank slate to work with, bolstering your confidence as you grow, or widen, your abilities.

If you're feeling pulled more towards the paranormal, or 'ghost hunting' there are many haunted locations which host tours and even private investigations where the staff will take you through the building. This removes the need for you to invest in expensive equipment or to travel the depths of haunted halls alone. Granted, some places will allow you to rent the location for just your group, but if that is a little beyond your comfort zone, sign up for an investigation with their staff until you are ready to try such a thing on your own.

There may even be a chance with the staff to roam on your own for a couple of hours, blending the two experiences.

The most important thing to remember with the paranormal, or haunted locations, is respect. Most of the time you are in their home, or at the most tragic, somewhere something horrible happened to them, perhaps even causing their deaths. When reaching out with your mediumship in such places be prepared for a rush of emotions, visions, voices and perhaps even being touched. Your vibrations are higher than the rest of the group touring the location. They will naturally seek your attention. How you react to these events will determine how the spirits there react to you. If your goal is to make communication, remember to try to react calmly. Even if you are in a state of panic, and want to run, as long as the interactions are not harmful, try to endure as long as you can to encourage them speaking with you. Should at any time the interactions are no longer welcomed, remember your boundaries. Either tell the spirit to step away or remove yourself from the situation completely. Should the atmosphere of the location seem to change to something unwelcoming, leave. Remember, you are the brightest light source in the room. Don't risk yourself by pushing the welcome of the spirits who are there. That won't end well for anyone. Plus, you can't expect spirits to respect your boundaries if you are not respecting theirs. The Conjuring House in Harrisville, Rhode Island is a perfect example of this. The spirits there are often very eager to make their presence known in a safe way, but should you test their welcome, you may discover yourself on the other side of their patience as few have discovered.

As a paranormal medium, as I prefer to label myself, I have explored many different locations with claims of being haunted from cemeteries, abandoned buildings and homes. I have even worked as caretakers, educating guests about the paranormal and the history of locations, as to why it might be haunted. Of course, I often wore every piece of grounding jewelry I owned in my practice to keep the energy at a level I could mentally sustain!

## PROTECT OUR BOUNDARIES

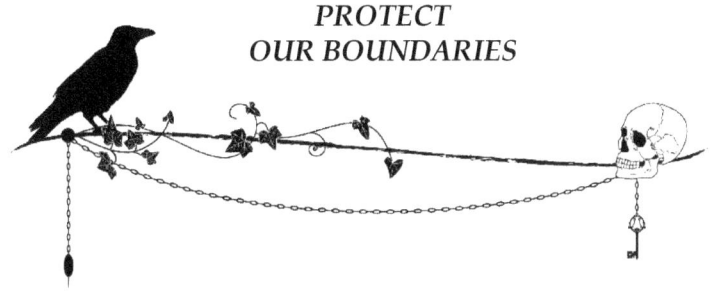

How do we open ourselves in such locations safely project our boundaries? Let's list a few examples.

****

***Speak with me, but respectfully.***

Before entering a location with claims of paranormal activity, sit in your vehicle for a few moments before exiting. The reason for this is you will most likely mentally feel safer in something which you is so familiar to you. It has nothing to do with the car being a source of protection other than your own energy filling it with trust.  You never want to step into a haunted location with anxiety. How you greet the space will be how it interacts with you if it's a malicious haunting. Remember your heart space meditation. Lift your confidence to have the power to put in place your boundaries.

This is also a suitable time to envision your space protected. Many use the white light method.

****

***Protect me with light.***

If you follow a path of religion, or walk with a Deity, call to them. Ask for them to be with you for the next few hours, or however long you intend to be at this location.

In your mind's eye, imagine a bright light starting in your heart, the strongest of your power sources. Ask your Divine, Spirit Guides and\or ancestors to fill that light, spreading it wide until it covers your whole body with protection. This is your shield keeping you safe with a metaphysical boundary. Whenever you feel this shield slipping, take a moment to refill it, asking our source of protection to help keep you safe.

Once you are ready to leave the location, send the white light on its way. Do not recall it back into yourself just in case there are any attachments you were being protected from. You can either send it into the ground or send it into the sky. Either way, send it away from you with thanks for its protection. This also infuses the space with love that others may draw on in their time of need.

*****

### *Anoint with fiery oils of protection.*

Just as using herbs to recharge your tools, it is possible to use oils to protect your energetic field. Holy Water is often used as it is universal for Christians. If not a Christian, there are plenty of options, as well. Oils holding patchouli, lavender, mugwort, hyssop, St. john's wort, blessed thistle and myrrh are some of the most popular ones and are the easiest to work with as far as their energy. These oils can be found at metaphysical stores with reputable reviews. Please do not leave your spiritual protection to unknown stores. You wouldn't trust just anyone with the health of your body. Please don't do the same with your spiritual health.

Personally, I anoint each of my chakra points with the oils, blocking all paths to my energy. I will also anoint the back of my head where the pituitary gland sits, as it is perceived to be the house of spiritual abilities. If you've ever entered a haunted location and felt the headache from the back of your head to the front, this is considered an activation of awareness to possible entities nearby you or where you are about to enter. Use this built-in alarm system until you have discovered your natural alarms to alert you to possibilities you are not alone.

I recommend if you are using the oils as a way to protect yourself to anoint often. Especially after an intense round of communication. When feeling more confident, you can blend oils for protection as well as clearing your mind for communication. Test the oils slowly to discover which blends work the best together and separately to see which works best for you.

Unlike with the white light method of protection, you do not need to worry about removing the oils before leaving the location. I would even leave the oils for several hours or until they dry on their own, keeping the barrier secure.

\*\*\*\*

## Let's Chat.

Some locations may be too intense for communication, or the communication may become too intense, but the interest is there to at least try to make communication. We will go back to our automatic writing practice. Let whatever words, feelings, visions you are sensing come freely to your mind. Don't communicate back. Just collect the information on the paper to be evaluated at a later time.

Sometimes spirits are over eager when they realize someone can hear them without the use of paranormal equipment. They will press heavily onto the medium, not always maliciously, but with over enthusiasm. Unfortunately for your energy it often feels the same. Once the initial rush is completed by the use of automatic writing, the energy will often ease away, allowing you to feel safe enough to communicate back with whomever is providing you with the information. If you feel safe enough to do after the first rush, now ask questions focused on the information you were first given to help put together what has been shown to you.

This, once again, is the point of boundaries. You are always in charge of the communication. Just as with someone who is verbally mistreating you, you would not sit and endure it. You have no obligation to do the same with spirits.

\*\*\*\*

*Crystals are a mediums' best friend.*

Not only can you wear crystals to protect yourself, but you can place them around an area you have set aside to work as a medium protecting the space you are in, as well. Using many of the ones we have already mentioned, place them in doorways and windowsills to be sure only the spirits you wish to speak with may enter your designated space. This will also limit the number of spirits in a space, so you do not become overwhelmed with their interest in you.

There is also always the possibility of placing them directly around you forming a tight grid around you and your group. If using paranormal equipment in tandem with the medium, remember to place the equipment outside of the grid. Otherwise, you may find the spirits are unable to manipulate the equipment due to the energy blocking them from getting too close to your group. As you are establishing your abilities, you most likely would like to be able to validate what you are being shown with equipment. Don't worry. Soon you won't care if the equipment coordinates, but it's always amusing for the skeptics when it does.

# Section Seven – The Road is Now Open

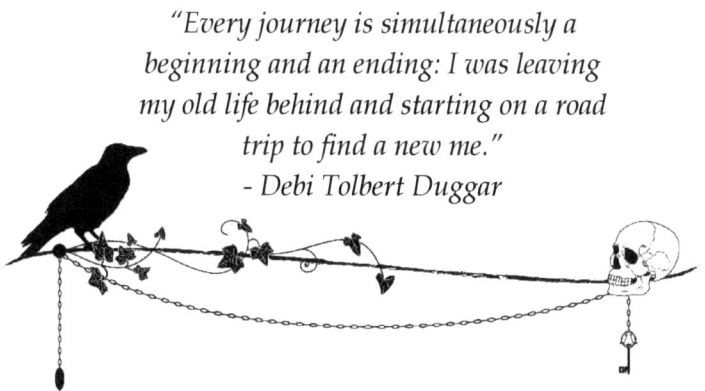

*"Every journey is simultaneously a beginning and an ending: I was leaving my old life behind and starting on a road trip to find a new me."*
- Debi Tolbert Duggar

Hopefully by now you have come to understand, even if you have never met someone like you, you are not alone. In fact, there are more of us with gifts than there are without gifts. The rarity is the fact that so few have the bravery to discover what the abilities truly are and the depths of where they could take someone. You, on the other hand, just by purchasing this book, are a rarity. You are the gem the veil is cheering for, someone who is afraid, but willing to explore their courage. If it's for you, or for your child, you are making a difference in the paranormal world, a world still very much a mystery to many.

Your journey will not be a straight path upon a paved road. It will be a wooded trail amid winding curves with slopes and hills. Despite your best efforts, not all communication will come easily. Just as in life, some are very chatty, some are too chatty and some just want to be left alone. Spirits are the same. It is best to start working with your Spirit Guides, Guardians and Ancestors before diving into the world of spirit communication. You would not dive into the deep end of the pool without some type of flotation device if you were not aware of how to swim. Please don't dive into the veil without some type of protection to keep you afloat.

Take this time to decide how you wish to travel forward. What type of mediumship do you feel most comfortable with? How do you receive your information in the ways you trust the most?

If it's divination, cards, palm reading, tea leaves, dowsing rods, so forth, find the tool which speaks to you, works with you and excites you. It should feel like an old friend every time you touch the tool. No fear and no judgement.

If it's mental, where you can hear, or see their messages, work to set your symbols into foundation. Develop what your symbol will be for a child, an adult, a father or mother and so forth. Allow these set symbols to guide your communication. This way no matter who you are speaking with, you will be able to understand what they are trying to tell you.

If it's trance, be sure your spiritual team is strong to protect you. Not only on the other side of the veil but also here on this side of the veil, as in your mediumship circle. Allow only those you trust to be in charge of the session since you, yourself, will be incapacitated during the event. This form is the hardest on the body so be sure to take care of yourself in every aspect for full, clear, evidence-based messages.

Perhaps you wish to speak to large crowds through gallery events. Be sure your boundaries are strong, letting the spirits know they may only come forward if for someone in the audience. Let them know you will only speak to one spirit at a time, so the messages don't get muddled. Be aware, this can take a mental toll with the sheer length of the channeling session. Once again, be sure your boundaries are intact, and your teams are prepared to help you should they be pressed upon.

No matter which road you choose to journey along, there will always be those ready to test you, mock you, and even berate you. Most do not come out as a medium with hopes of becoming rich. It is not an easy role in this life. While, if used correctly, can be a noble profession, there are much easier jobs, or even hobbies.

Never allow anyone to mock your journey. Even if it's a client, you have the right to close the session at any time. No one has the right to belittle you. Nor do you have the right to mock them for not believing in you for it is not your purpose to try to convince someone to believe in you. Either they will, or they won't. It's not your worry.

So, what happens when you have made your mind upon this path and it's all going wrong? You've been successful with evidential mediumship in the past. Why now is it going wrong? *Is it* going wrong? Your ability to share the message is only as strong as the connection the spirit has with you at that moment. Perhaps you are tired that day. Perhaps the client isn't willing to hear what you are saying or only wants to speak with a particular spirit which isn't making their presence known during the appointment. This is not a reflection of your abilities. No medium is ever always correct. You will have bad days, weak connections, incorrect messages and unreasonable appointments. It's not an 'if'. It's a 'when.'

After one of these days take some time to reconnect yourself with your team. Check in with yourself. Has some unresolved shadow work arrived? Have you been pushing yourself too hard? Are you bringing your personal drama into session, dimming your vibrations so they cannot lift to the frequency they need to? Take the time to discover this. Be honest with yourself for the other side will see through any lies you tell yourself and they may become unwilling to work with you.

In parting, understand there are many distinct aspects of mediumship. If I were to fill them all in one book it would become overwhelming. The core aspects of stepping out into the world is to be prepared for the hardships. Understand not many will cheer for you along this rutted path. You may lose friends, family members and comforts of the day-to-day life.

For those with children learning their abilities, other parents will question you as to why you allow your child to believe in nonsense. They will give well-meaning advice on handling the nightmares, stories about dead relatives or even the predictions upon strangers' lives. Your friends may discourage you from allowing them to speak with their "invisible friends" to the point of asking you both to not come around anymore. Parenthood is never easy. It's one of the most challenging roles anyone may ever have, but knowing you are doing right for your child is the most important role of life. By standing by your child's side, you may very well be saving their life. The rate of suicides among child mediums is staggering. They need you, even if you don't understand, however they will allow you to help, they need you.

Witchcraft has helped me understand my purpose and journey. That doesn't mean it is the only path forward. There are plenty of spiritual churches who blend mediumship with religion, where one is not judged but accepted for their abilities. They will often times hold gallery events and mediumship circles. Explore what fits you best to aid you. Feeling safe and secure will be the biggest advantage to expanding your understanding of what you are capable of doing.

I decided to pick up the caldron, so to say, due to certain members of my family denouncing me and calling me a witch for hearing the voices and seeing spirits. I knew I was never going to change their minds. To this day I still wonder how someone who proclaims to be Christian can hate someone so much for their own personal path, but I suppose there are a lot of us with that question for varied reasons. The pain will always be there. The pain of knowing your own blood refuses you, but as often repeated - The blood of the covenant is thicker than the blood of the womb. No one, not even your own family, has the right to hurt you. Perhaps, like myself, you walked this razor blade of false grass so you might one day be the light for another.

Let your light shine. There is enough darkness in the world, already. The witch I am, sees the power in you and I hope. I pray, that you too will come to see it in time. Until then, you are not alone. You just haven't found us, yet.

# Appendix

*"Always remember the answers come
not from the rock, the teacup, the shell, or the cards.
The answers come from you."*
*- Gwendolyn Womack*

**Pick a card any card or pendulum or dowsing rod or spirit board or rune or……**

Divination pairs perfectly with mediumship. Learning to trust what you are seeing and hearing with the use of your favorite tool builds confidence in blooming abilities, but it can be intimidating to figure out which tool will pair best with not only your abilities but also with your energy. There are amazing card readers, but they flop when it comes to runes. Perhaps spirit boards feel perfect but dowsing rods make you feel silly. There is no perfect tool. The answers come from your abilities. The tools just help you fine tune your gifts until you are ready to walk without them.

I remember the first time I walked into a metaphysical store. It felt as if I was breaking every rule my family had forced upon me. This is a store of Devil worship, after all. Just walking through the door means I am running the risk of condemning my soul. There might be no amount of repenting I could do to save myself and here I was with the goal of buying cards.

I wore large sunglasses. Spoke with almost no one as I browsed the many shelves of brightly colored boxes. I didn't listen to my team. I didn't listen to my intuition. I just wanted to get out of there before the guilt of being in the store swallowed me whole right on the spot. I made the same mistake a lot of people make when they are starting out without support. I grabbed a box which looked the prettiest, paid for it, and ran out of the door to the safety of my car where I felt I could breathe again.

Once home, I opened the cards like a child trying to avoid being caught doing something naughty. I was almost giggling with the feeling of rebellion the act was supplying me. As if this small box was the answer I was looking for, I thought these paper rectangles were going to allow everything to make sense. A bright moment of 'aha' was about to happen for me, but it didn't. I felt just as lost as I frantically shuffled and followed recommended spread after spread with my newly purchased oracle deck. The cheerful cards with their words of encouragement placed under the art left me with more questions than answers. I felt devastated.

I had made the same mistake many make when they are starting to explore divination. I bought based off eagerness and not what would be useful to my energy. I was so excited to get started on the path I didn't take the time to explore the path first.

That deck still sits amid the many I have collected for different reasons through the years. I have tried to reconnect with it many times, but, unfortunately, it still does not mesh with my energy. It actually became the starter deck for my daughter until she expanded into other tools. I still have respect for that deck. It might not have been able to answer questions I proposed to it, but it did teach me a lesson about myself and divination.

In time, I found the decks which spoke to me energetically and visually. I still use them to this day with clients in conjunction with tarot cards and other tools depending on the reading. This is why so many love cards as their source of divination. They pair very well with almost every other form as either support or the main theme to a session.

As much as I love them, they are not for everyone so please don't feel pressured to rush out and find your first deck. I also love my spirit board for seances. My pendulums for quick answers and dowsing rods for paranormal investigations. Each tool has their use in my life, but it always comes back to the same lesson – Are you picking for eagerness or are you picking the tool which fits?

I am going to go over some of the most popular divination tools in the next few pages to help you decide which might be best for you. Don't worry if more than one piques your interest. My working space holds a bit of everything as I never know what I may be called on to help someone with so don't feel worried about confining yourself to just one tool. Confession: most mediums have more tools then they will ever need.

# PICKING YOUR FIRST SPIRITUAL BEST FRIEND

It can feel overwhelming when you first step into a metaphysical store. A good store invested in the aspects of spirituality should be able to provide you with a wide range of tools to explore. There should be a variety of cards, pendulums, spirit boards, runes and other forms of divination. Some may be considered tabooer than others such as bones and spirit boards, but I don't want you to shy away from them due to popular opinions. We will go through each tool so you will feel confident about your choice.

\*\*\*\*

## Oracle Cards and Angel Cards

Most people will start with this type of divination. These decks hold less cards than tarot cards. Since they also have their own meanings, it removes the need to memorize their meanings. This allows for less intimidation for beginners and is a comfort factor for those who use them. Now, by no means does this ever mean you have to move from them. There are many amazing readers who I know who use oracle and angel cards with their clients. This all comes back to what meshes with your energy and your spiritual team. Never feel less of a reader if this is what you choose to use for your divination.

How do you pick your deck? This is sometimes tricky. Even the best of decks can prove to be disappointing when trying to connect with them. How does the artwork make you feel? Does it match your personality? What about the messages on the cards? Do they match advice you would give friends? These are key factors to making sure you pick a deck to work with either professionally or for yourself.

Now unfortunately you can follow all this advice and still you won't feel a connection to them when the time comes to use them. It happens. There are others who suggest keeping the cards on you as you go about your day to charge them to your energy or to sleep with them under your pillow. I don't follow any of this philosophy. Not that it's wrong. It's just not in my nature to force a relationship with my tools. In some cases, the decks which didn't work, or vibe, upon their purchase will suddenly click days or weeks later. When this happens for me, I take it as a hint my main decks need a vacation and have called in backup!

****

### Tarot Cards

Tarot cards are the industry standard. Most shows and movies always portray this rather intense spread of cards and someone mystically reading them. Despite all the intimidation surrounding them, they really are not as complicated as some readers, and Hollywood, would love for you to believe. If you feel tarot cards are the path for you, use the same advice above to pick your first deck, but most will recommend you start with some from of the standard Rider-Waite deck to help with the memorization of the cards many meanings through the understood artwork and symbols. I still use forms of this deck with my clients as it is the most recognized form of tarot.

There are plenty of classes offered on how to read tarot cards from free on YouTube to paid classes online and in person. I even teach classes at my shop in Rhode Island – Great Hexpectations.

I personally cannot tell you every meaning of every card. I read the cards intuitively with my guides as help to interpret the cards for the person sitting for their appointment. I don't hold hard to the card's meanings, as some readers believe they should be read. Trust your team and your own intuition as to how you will move forward with your cards.

****

## Pendulums

I love my pendulums the way some women love shoes. I have one for every occasion. Sean considers it amusing I cannot go to a store without finding a new pendulum to adopt. Nor can I restrain myself when it's time to restock them in our shop. With as many uses as they can provide, I always suggest having one in your spiritual toolbox.

I have pendulums for paranormal investigations. I have ones to use with clients who need a simple yes\no answer. I have them for Reiki sessions to test the flow of energy so I can quickly see where and what is blocked. I have pendulums associated with the Deities I work with allowing me to have direct communication with them as well pendulums for my ancestors when I need more earthly advice. They are all different materials from copper for paranormal to crystals for Reiki. This is a personal preference and for me I try to match the material to the job I have for the pendulum.

You can discover which pendulum will work with you much easier than a card deck. The correct pendulum will vibrate in response to your energy by placing your hand under it. Even the slightest movement can be interpreted as a 'yes' response to willingness to work with you. To further test its willingness, ask for it to show you how it will move when the answer is 'yes'. Repeat but ask which movement will be for 'no'. Now, it will be exciting to see this move of its own accord, but test how it feels in your hand. Wrap the chain around your fingers to judge the weight of it as it hangs freely. It should feel comfortable to hold it because you may find yourself holding it for a while depending on for what you may be using it. Once again, listen to your intuition and the practicality of the item. Don't be like me and adopt it simply because you have to have it. At least not starting out. There will be plenty of time to hoard divination tools as you progress along your path. I promise.

****
## Runes

Runes are a form of alphabet forming individual symbols, or characters, to represent sounds and meanings. The most common runes, the ones often found at metaphysical stores, are made from the Elder Futhark alphabet. They consist normally of 24 pieces and can be made from bones, to wood, to crystal and even plaster. Much like cards, it's really up to you and what meshes with your energy as to which ones to choose to work with in your divination. If feeling very brave, you can make your own with wood or stones you find amid your day-to-day life.

Runes and I have never connected. Remember when I said there are great card readers, but they flop with Runes? That's me. I have tried several times to work with them many times, but they are just not for me. I find runes to be one of the harder forms of divination to master and am always impressed when I see someone proficient with them.

I have heard the best way to pick your runes is to hold them in your hands. If the bag feels heavy, they are not for you. If the bag feels light, this is a set which may work with your energy. After all, you have to feel comfortable casting them to allow the spreads to reveal the answers.

****
## The Darker Arts

There are those who think of spirit boards, or Ouija boards, as gateways to evil. Please remember, any divination tool you use is in all technicalities is opening a 'gateway'. By asking your team, Spirit Guides, ancestors and even Guardian Angels to step close to you, you are creating a 'gateway'. The difference is Hollywood has made millions from convincing people these boards are somehow more potent with negative energy just waiting to jump out and possess you. After all, a horror movie about a pendulum would not be as impressive or one featuring the many paper cuts a reader can receive from cards during a long day at an event. As a professional reader, I am way more terrified of what my tarot cards and bones will say to me than what my spirit board might. Especially the bones. Nothing holds more soul crushing answers than the bones.

I would caution the use of a spirit board until you are comfortable with your spiritual team to protect you. Especially since, in essence, the board is used to communicate with the dead and not your spiritual team for advice. There are certain 'rules' and etiquette understood with the board. Honestly, just like any other tool, the board will let you know how it wants to be treated and used better than any rule book one might present you with. You are giving energy to an item and that energy will gladly show itself in time letting you discover its personality.

1. Do not leave the planchette on the board when finished. You need to be sure the session has come to a complete end to not have the dead sitting there listening to elevator music as they wait for your next communication. If you make a habit of this, the helpful dead won't want to pick up the line when you call if you are already leaving them on hold. When you are through with the session, store the planchette somewhere safe and with respect. I wrap mine in a velvet pouch.

2. Try not to use the board alone. This is not due to the fear of possession. It is difficult to remember each letter as the dead are exerting their energy to move the planchette. You will find yourself with false letters, words, or worse, having to ask them to try again. This is like going to the gym and your personal trainer keeps asking you to redo sets of pushups because they weren't paying attention. It's only a matter of time till the dead become annoyed and refuse to communicate with you any further leaving you to believe your board no longer works. The reopening of the board ritual, which I will cover

in another book, can become tedious if you keep chasing away the dead.

3. If you're going to use the board as a form of divination, and not just for decoration, it should be treated with the same respect as your other divination tools. Do not let others fool around with it. Do not use it when bored and friends are over to scare each other. Do not move the planchette on your own to achieve answers for amusement. This will build mistrust with the dead who will refuse to work with you.

Whereas most of this seems like common sense, I wanted to add it to be sure one understands how to effectively use a spirit board. I use mine when doing seances and because I have shown the dead the proper respect with the board, they are willing, and eager, to work with it. Please remember any time you are inviting the dead to speak with you to have your boundaries firmly established and protection in place.

****

### Mirror Scrying

There are several different ways to perform mirror scrying. There is the style of sitting with a candle, staring at the candle's flame in the reflection with a soft gaze until you begin to see figures, or shapes, appear in the glass of the mirror. For someone with a short attention span like me, this is torture.

Instead, I use a trifold mirror behind me as I sit in front of a mirror with a candle. This allows my attention span to gaze in several different mirrors while performing this divination. I teach mirror scrying this way in my classes, as well. It's just easier. Not everything has to be over complicated and mystical. Do what works.

Make sure you have a journal nearby to write down anything which happens during the sessions. We have a way of forgetting details once we step back into this realm with its many needs for our attention. Plus, the excitement one feels the first time it works also tends to blur our memory as we wonder if it was real or just our imagination playing tricks on us.

There is also black mirror scrying. In this process you have painted mirrors completely black with the candlelight becoming more of a glow which can often times be manipulated by spirits to form shapes to communicate with you. Start with the first. Then move to black mirrors. Keep a journal of your progress so you may celebrate your success.

****

### Dowsing Rods

Yes, some consider dowsing rods to be on the more risker side of divination tools, believe it or not. These copper rods were originally intended to find sources of water and even blood to help find wounded soldiers in wars who may have crawled from the battlefield for safety. Today they are used often for spirit communication.

There really is no limit to how dowsing rods can be used to receive messages. Of course, there is the amazingly simple yes/no, but there is so much more to what these simple tools can provide for you. I have LED rods which I use at night to be easily seen because spirits can use them to show you items, or locations they wish you to visit if you choose to work at haunted locations. For example, The Conjuring House spirits love to show you directions to hidden graves and I have used the rods when finding myself lost in the woods to find my way back to the house. Please remember if you are going to go out into deserted locations, don't trust just the rods to lead you to safety. Just with all types of divination you never know who might decide to come play with you. Especially when it comes to entities of the land. You don't want to pick up a trickster with hopes they are leading you home when instead they are having a field day getting you lost and deeper into trouble.

If you wish to learn a spirit's name, have it cross when you reach the letter of the alphabet which belongs to them. You can do the same with their age, when they were born and even the date of their death.

You can also ask them to spin one rod to equal the number of years they were before they died or another other number you are looking to learn such as children, siblings, etc.

My favorite when leading spirit investigation is to ask spirit to move one rod to show where they are standing, who their favorite guest is, who their least favorite guest is, and my favorite, which guest will cause me the most trouble of the night. Watching skeptics' eyes as the spirits play duck-duck-goose with the guests is always fun to behold.

Please explore all the many ways dowsing rods work. Do not limit this amazing tool to just yes/no, cheating yourself out of mind-blowing information they can provide during an investigation.

To find your perfect set, practice holding them with relaxed shoulders and elbows tucked to your sides. The rods should be able to sway easily but also not so easily they move out of control. Test to see the weight of the rods. Depending on what they are made of, some can be very cumbersome to hold for long durations, such as my LED ones. Just as with the pendulum test, ask the rods to show you their yes/no motions. If there is hesitation, or a disconnect, these may not be the set for you. If determined, I have found dowsing rods are the easiest of all tools to build a working relationship with should you decide to put the time in with a particular set. I have never had dowsing rods refuse to collaborate with me. They might be on the cold shoulder for a little while but they always eagerly come around when shown the proper respect.

****

These are just a few of the many tools available for you which are easily found to start to work with in your journey. Explore as many as you feel pulled towards. There is no need to limit yourself to just one tool. Especially since most tools love to work together to provide you with a wide picture of life.

Remember, when in doubt, always reach out to someone you trust to answer any questions which may come up when working with your tools. Most importantly remember you are the source of the information. The tools are just training wheels until you are ready to fully embrace your mediumship.

In time you won't need tools at all. You'll start to 'hear' the information before your tools can express it. Tools are simply a way to reinforce what you are feeling, hearing, or seeing along your journey. Some Mediums still use their tools even at a professional level. Most times it's for the crowd, or client, and not for themselves. Either way, do what makes you feel confident as that is the trick to all of this.

You have to be willing to trust what you are feeling to fully be open to mediumship and the craft. The two are so intermingled they are almost impossible to separate. From simple things such as lighting candles for the dead to full seances, it is all aspects of the craft. Some just feel comfortable giving their practice different names – which is fine. It's your journey.

If you take nothing at all away from this book, take at least the understanding you are loved. You are loved by generations of those who came before you. They are always working to help you behind the scenes to allow your life to be easier, even if it doesn't always feel that way.

Your guides are always with you. You are never truly alone. You are so loved. So perfect. And life can truly be whatever you make it if you have the desire to try. I believe you do, and I believe in you. Wherever you are, whoever you are, I believe in you. Your spiritual team believes in you. We are all so eager to meet you, cheer for you and be happy for you that you took this journey and were not left to the shadows of your lost potential.

Until then, we will wait for you.

Hope to meet you soon,

Maria Dorgan as Marie F Crow

# About the Author

Maria and Sean work constantly to help those discover their spiritual gifts in Coventry, Rhode Island. Together, they have built a community of like-minded individuals at their location, Great Hexpectations and through Maria's podcast featured on Spotify, Great Hexpectations, The Witch I Am.

Through lectures and classes they are showing the world Mediumship is not something one should fear but embrace. With many stories matching Marie's, they strive to help those who have been wounded to heal and come to love their light once again.

Sean is often heard telling those around them, "If you need help, let us know. We might not be able to fix everything, but we can show you a path to healing which is the start of everything."

# Also by the Author

**The Risen Series**
Dawning
Margaret
Remnants
Courage
Defiance

**A Risen Series Novel**
Genny
Lost Doves (Coming Soon)

**The Siren Series**
Crown of Betrayal
Crown of Remorse
Crown of Conquest
Crown of Secrets (Coming Soon)

**The Great Hexpectation Series**
The Little Lies
The Broken Hearted
The Whispered Words (Coming Soon)

**The Abigail and her Pet Zombie Series**
*Illustrated Children's Books*
Abigail and her Pet Zombie
Zoo Day
Spring
Summer
Halloween
Happy Birthday
A Very Zombie Christmas
Valentine's Day (Coming Soon)

**The Abigail and her Pet Zombie Series**
*Beginner Chapter Books*
Abigail and her Pet Zombie

**The Unwanted Series**
The Great Adventure (Coming Soon)

## Podcast

Listen Now!

# Where to find the Author?

**GREAT HEXPECTATIONS**
ECLECTIC SPIRITUAL STORE

501 Washington St
Coventry RI 02816

Great Hexpectations:
www.facebook.com/GreatHexpectations

Marie F. Crow
www.facebook.com/MarieFCrow.Author

## About the Publisher

Kingston Publishing Company, founded by C. K. Green, is dedicated to providing authors an affordable way to turn their dream into a reality. We publish over 100+ titles annually in multiple formats including print and ebook across all major platforms.

We offer every service you will ever need to take an idea and publish a story. We are here to help authors make it in the industry. We want to provide a positive experience that will keep you coming back to us. Whether you want a traditional publisher who offers all the amenities a publishing company should or an author who prefers to self-publish, but needs additional help – we are here for you.

Now Accepting Manuscripts!
Please send query letter and manuscript to:
submissions@kingstonpublishing.com

Visit our website at
www.kingstonpublishing.com

www.ingramcontent.com/pod-product-compliance
Lightning Source LLC
Chambersburg PA
CBHW061748070526
44585CB00025B/2837